Praise for *The Best American Poetry*

"Each year, a vivid snapshot of what a distinguished poet finds exciting, fresh, and memorable: and over the years, as good a comprehensive overview of contemporary poetry as there can be."

—Robert Pinsky

"The *Best American Poetry* series has become one of the mainstays of the poetry publication world. For each volume, a guest editor is enlisted to cull the collective output of large and small literary journals published that year to select seventy-five of the year's 'best' poems. The guest editor is also asked to write an introduction to the collection, and the anthologies would be indispensable for these essays alone; combined with [David] Lehman's 'state-of-poetry' forewords and the guest editors' introductions, these anthologies seem to capture the zeitgeist of the current attitudes in American poetry."

—Academy of American Poets

"A high volume of poetic greatness . . . in all of these volumes . . . there is brilliance, there is innovation, there are surprises."

—*The Villager*

"A year's worth of the very best!"

—*People*

"A preponderance of intelligent, straightforward poems."

—*Booklist*

"Certainly it attests to poetry's continuing vitality."

—*Publishers Weekly* (starred review)

"A 'best' anthology that really lives up to its title."

—*Chicago Tribune*

"An essential purchase."

—*The Washington Post*

OTHER VOLUMES IN THIS SERIES

THE
BEST
AMERICAN
POETRY
2015

◇ ◇ ◇

Sherman Alexie, Editor

David Lehman, Series Editor

SCRIBNER POETRY

NEW YORK   LONDON   TORONTO   SYDNEY   NEW DELHI

Scribner Poetry
An Imprint of Simon & Schuster, Inc.
1230 Avenue of the Americas
New York, NY 10020

First Scribner hardcover edition September 2015

SCRIBNER and design are registered trademarks of The Gale Group, Inc., used under license by Simon & Schuster, Inc., the publisher of this work.

For information about special discounts for bulk purchases, please contact Simon & Schuster Special Sales at 1-866-506-1949 or business@simonandschuster.com.

The Simon & Schuster Speakers Bureau can bring authors to your live event. For more information or to book an event, contact the Simon & Schuster Speakers Bureau at 1-866-248-3049 or visit our website at www.simonspeakers.com.

Manufactured in the United States of America

1   3   5   7   9   10   8   6   4   2

Library of Congress Control Number: 88644281

ISBN 978-1-4767-0819-5
ISBN 978-1-4767-0820-1 (pbk.)
ISBN 978-1-4767-0821-8 (ebook)

CONTENTS

David Lehman was born in New York City. Educated at Stuyvesant High School and Columbia University, he spent two years as a Kellett Fellow at Clare College, Cambridge, and worked as Lionel Trilling's research assistant upon his return from England. He is the author of nine books of poetry, including *New and Selected Poems* (2013), *When a Woman Loves a Man* (2005), *The Daily Mirror* (2000), and *Valentine Place* (1996), all from Scribner. He is the editor of *The Oxford Book of American Poetry* (Oxford, 2006) and *Great American Prose Poems: From Poe to the Present* (Scribner, 2003), among other collections. Two prose books appeared in 2015: *The State of the Art: A Chronicle of American Poetry, 1988–2014* (Pittsburgh), comprising all the forewords he has written for *The Best American Poetry*, and *Sinatra's Century: One Hundred Notes on the Man and His World* (HarperCollins). *A Fine Romance: Jewish Songwriters, American Songs* (Nextbook/Schocken) won the Deems Taylor Award from the American Society of Composers, Authors, and Publishers (ASCAP) in 2010. He teaches in the graduate writing program of The New School and lives in New York City and in Ithaca, New York.

FOREWORD

by David Lehman

◊　◊　◊

When you write an annual column for nearly three decades, you may, in effect, be writing a book in discontinuous increments. But you're not necessarily conscious of it. You don't consult the previous year's report before writing the present one, so when you put them together and reread the lot, you're likely to be in for a few surprises.

In 2015 the twenty-nine "forewords" that had appeared to date in *The Best American Poetry* were gathered in *The State of the Art: A Chronicle of American Poetry, 1988–2014* and published by the University of Pittsburgh Press. Rereading the pieces in consecutive order, I was struck not only by unconscious repetitions (Wordsworth on pleasure and the formation of poetic taste, "abundance" as the defining trait of American poetry, W. H. Auden's observations, Oscar Wilde's paradoxes) but also, for example, by my evident partiality for the "not only/but also" rhetorical formula.

My pet peeves never let me down. I seem always to have been aghast at ad hoc pronouncements that pass for critical judgments and can rarely let it go unremarked when somebody lowers the limbo bar even in the act of elegizing some aspect of the poetry he despises. The December 2014 issue of *The Atlantic* provided a perfect illustration: a piece by James Parker lamenting, in the year of the Welsh poet's centenary, the loss of Dylan Thomas. The article's title states the theme: "The Last Rock-Star Poet."[1] As the last of that Bardic breed, Thomas (Parker says) was worthy of our attention if not our unequivocal acclaim—except that as a poet he didn't amount to all that much. In Parker's words, "'Fern Hill' is gloop; 'Do not go gentle into that good night' is inferior Yeats." That sentence, those judgments, are backed up by nothing. They are not even discussed, let alone substantiated, explained, argued. They

---

1. James Parker, "The Last Rock-Star Poet," *The Atlantic*, December 2014, pp. 50–52.

are merely stated as if they were beyond dispute—articles of received wisdom elevated to self-evident propositions. I wondered whether the writer had taken the time to reread "Fern Hill" or was he merely, as was possible, revolted by the memory of a younger version of himself, who had a deep crush on Thomas, having been smitten, as he admits, by "the charm of the man, the charm of the boy, the shock-headed cherub-troll who'd come waddling down to London from Swansea with a cigarette between his lips and a brown beer bottle in his pocket."

"Fern Hill" is a full-throated evocation of Edenic innocence, a Romantic recollection of an enchanted boyhood in the tradition variously exemplified by Thomas Traherne in the latter half of the seventeenth century and Wordsworth a century later. I like quoting the last three lines of the poem because they reach for the highest notes available in bringing this elegy for youth to a close:

> Oh as I was young and easy in the mercy of his means,
> Time held me green and dying
> Though I sang in my chains like the sea.

Is it possible that these lines make *The Atlantic* writer gag ("gloop") precisely because they are so rich and so affecting and because such qualities are as outmoded as neckties? The sheer passion of the writing; the artful repetition of key phrases introduced earlier ("young and easy," "Time" as a divine agent); the complexity of the final utterance, a subordinate clause that surpasses the main clause in its lyricism; the arresting simile at the very end—there is wizardry here, and wonderment, a sense of the natural sublime.

As for "Do not go gentle into that good night," to dismiss Thomas's famous villanelle as "inferior Yeats" is a pedantry, and a false one. Use Yeats as your standard, and few poets shall 'scape whipping. But for the record Yeats did not write villanelles, and the effects Thomas achieves in "Do not go gentle" are not those that the Irish poet was after. In the face of his father's imminent demise, Thomas used the constrictive form dialectically, to discipline his feelings and to apply a restraint on his fountain of imagery and linguistic genius. The poem's second stanza attests to the power that he achieved through the use of the strict form:

> Though wise men at their end know dark is right,
> Because their words had forked no lightning they
> Do not go gentle into that good night.

This is not a brand of poetry that would please the British poets of ironic understatement who chose Hardy as a master and whose greatest practitioner is Larkin. But it is a sterling example of Thomas's method, which (he wrote in a letter) was to let one image "breed another, let that image contradict the first, make, of the third image bred out of the other two together, a fourth contradictory image, and let them all, within my imposed formal limits, conflict." The method is at the service of something that can never stay out of fashion for long: the heroic note, defiance in the face of mortality.

Instant dismissal of greatness goes together with a second thing that reliably gets a rise out of me, the glorification of dumbness in American culture. A generously funded study indicates that there is a correlation between the elimination of course requirements and widespread ignorance of American history, civics, our government and economic structures. Although you might expect to see such a revelation in a satirical weekly, it gets half a page of a daily newspaper noted for its sobriety. Some readers may wonder whether we really need focus groups, task forces, or in this case a commissioned study to reveal what anecdotal evidence provides in abundance—or perhaps this academic exercise in stating the obvious itself lends credence to the argument. In any case, if you wanted the veneer of pseudo-scientific authority that only statistics can confer, you are now entitled to say that most college students do not know the length of a congressman's term, the meaning and purpose of the Emancipation Proclamation, or the name of the Revolutionary War general in charge of American forces at Yorktown.[2]

As if to signal its opposition to grade inflation—another villain in parables about the decline of an informed citizenry—the American Council of Trustees and Alumni has issued grades to universities and colleges. Both Wesleyan University, whose president has written in passionate defense of the humanities, and Brown University, that bastion of exclusive progressivism, were among the ninety-eight institutions that flunked. Fewer than one in five graduates of F-rated schools will have been required to take a class in American history. Even fewer will have been asked to study a foreign language or Economics 101. As one who loved his Columbia education, with its strong core requirements, it pains me that our graduates know less, and are expected to know less, than their counterparts in previous generations. It is as though the

2. Douglas Belkin, "For College Students, History's a Mystery," *The Wall Street Journal*, October 15, 2014, p. A6.

entire teaching profession has adopted a version of magical thinking that allows everyone to spin off the responsibility. But this I know: A lack of conviction in what you are teaching spells disaster. As Magdalena Kay writes: "Our current sense of crisis is partly a crisis of faith in what we are teaching, not just in how we are teaching it."[3] Kay quotes Christopher Lasch, prophet of *The Culture of Narcissism*: "When elders make no demands on the young, they make it almost impossible for the young to grow up."

Poetry may be the enchanted childhood, the "farm forever fled" in Dylan Thomas's ode to a lost paradise. But poetry is also an essential part of adulthood, and adulthood a more serious state of mind and being than an adolescence idealized by an eighteenth-century savant. I will continue to speak up for such allegedly outmoded things as canonical books, the study of Western culture and modern thought, the concept of genius, the value of the memorization and recital of verse, the sustaining power of the imagination, and the privileged status of the aesthetic considered apart from all political considerations. To an extent I believe that the attachment to such cultural values puts one in opposition to the worship of handheld gadgetry. I will always favor the physical book, but it would be foolish to deny a changing actuality— and the benefits that come with it. While I don't find it natural to read, say, George Meredith's *Modern Love* online, I am glad this formerly hard-to-find sequence of poems is available there, and I believe, moreover, that it is useless to resist advances in technological efficiency. The medium may not be the message but it alters the ground conditions of its being.

The idea of using social media as a channel for poetry has its attractions. Robert Wilson, editor of *The American Scholar*, initiated "Next Line, Please" on the magazine's website and asked me to serve as quizmaster and prompt-maker. Since we began the weekly challenges in May 2014, we crowd-sourced a rhymed sonnet over the course of fifteen weeks; we then had competitions for best haiku, tanka, anagram, limerick, sestina, completion of a fragment by Emily Dickinson, opening and closing sentences of imaginary novels. Among my favorites was the one we devoted to couplets. Each entry had to have "fall" as an end-word, with the result that seven of the couplets, when combined, fulfilled the requirements of two forms—the ghazal and the sonnet, or

3. *The American Scholar*, Spring 2013, p. 38; p. 43.

what Mariam Zafar dubbed the "ghazal sonnet." Here's what we came up with:

The better the book, the longer the farewell,
the leaves in amber as their shadows fall.

With a red gold fire raining down, we fall
in love. The lonely branches sprawling tall,

We lug the red-leaf-laden tarp like pall-
bearers to curbs for trucks to haul away our fall.

Of all sad leaves that curl and fall,
the red are those I must recall.

My austral spring belies your boreal fall;
you burn brown leaves and dismiss my call.

On the yellow brick road to Damascus St. Paul took a fall,
as did Bogart in *To Have and Have Not* upon meeting Bacall.

Popeye chuckled and scratched his balls: on the wall
he scrawled, "Explore the mall in the reddening fall."

The authors were Bruce Bond, Katie Naoum, Leonard Kress, Lawrence Epstein, Diana (no last name given), Terence Winch, and John Tranter (channeling John Ashbery).

"Next Line, Please" was just one of several online verse initiatives that got started in 2014. *The New York Times* launched "The New Verse News" in December 2014. Poets were approached and asked to contribute a poem based on their reading of the day's newspaper. I was invited, and on Monday the 22nd, I wrote a poem based on the front-page article "Accusers and the Accused, Crossing Paths at Columbia" by Ariel Kaminer. This well-researched piece about tensions on the campus of my alma mater made me ponder the conflicts revealed and the mysteries stated but unsolved.[4] Lifting whole phrases from the article, I wrote this:

4. Ariel Kaminer, "Accusers and the Accused, Crossing Paths at Columbia," *The New York Times*, December 22, 2014, p. 1.

Accusers and the Accused, Crossing Paths at Columbia

False reports of rape are rare.
The accused rapist, an architecture student from Germany, said
"My mother raised me as a feminist."
He supports equal rights for women.
Three women have accused him of "intimate partner violence."

One accuser takes a bed with her wherever she goes
Which doubles as her senior thesis
And, in October, students at more than 100 colleges
Carried a mattress or pillow to dramatize the crisis
Of sexual assault on campus.

The president said "law and the principles of academic freedom
And at the same time protecting the rights of all."

The man in the watch cap sits on the steps of Low Library.
He said it didn't happen.
Most of his friends dropped him
Last year when Ms. Sulkowicz—
Or when the *Spectator* published his name.
Campus hearings have a lower burden of proof
Than criminal trials and he said he was not allowed.
But she did not press criminal charges.

None of them would ever get over it.

Though I did little more than rearrange choice parts of the article, making a few changes in wording and adding the final line, the editor in charge of "New Verse News" informed me that the paper's "top editors along with the lawyers" decided against running the poem "given the sensitivities involved." The subject was too hot to handle in a poem. The decision surprised me, because my poem did not strike me as either particularly provocative or deliberately offensive. Maybe, I mused, the editors thought the poem was boring. But a wise friend countered that if it had been boring, the paper would have unhesitatingly posted it. No, I am afraid that the key words were "lawyers" and "sensitivities." The lesson, so far as I can see, is that what is acceptable in a fact-checked newspaper article becomes dangerous, or potentially dangerous, in a poem—even if the poem is absolutely faithful to the facts as reported. A poem is not a straightforward article; its meaning is not self-evident; it can be ambiguous, and if it is, it is dangerous, the more so at a time when the "sensitivities" of special-interest groups play a decisive part in limiting free speech on campus and everywhere else. From the newspaper's point of view, there was only a downside in posting my poem. They had wanted something harmless, or funny, or "poetic," not anything that could stir up emotions about such timely campus subjects as rape and sexual assault, "yes means yes" contracts preceding the consummation of an affair, the rights of the accused in rape cases, the effects on the accusers, the artwork as a substitute for a conventional "senior thesis," the way language reflects these tensions, the resort to platitudes by the university leadership.

I do not want to inflate the importance of my poem's fate. In journalism these things happen all the time. But a larger problem bedevils us: the problem of censorship and self-censorship. In 2014 hackers purportedly on hire from North Korea made a cyber raid on the electronic coffers of Sony Pictures. The hack attack was sparked by the studio's intention to release a broad comedy starring Seth Rogen and James Franco as a pair of journalists who are recruited to assassinate the leader of North Korea. It resulted in much egg on the face and a big hole in Sony's pocketbook. But the violation of Sony's cyberspace also delivered an unsubtle threat. Theater chains in the United States refused to book *The Interview*, not because it was a lousy film but out of fear that some madman might bring an AK-47 to the mall and mow down customers. Sony withdrew the picture; President Obama rebuked Sony and promised to retaliate for the act of "cyber vandalism," and the leader of North Korea labeled our president a "monkey." For a while George Clooney couldn't get anywhere with a petition urging solidarity with the makers of the movie, and though the film was released in the end, if only in a limited way, what bothered fans of the First Amendment was how quickly and instinctively we and our institutions cave in to the demands of dictators, even those of the tinpot variety.

The willingness to button up our lips does nothing to deter such shocking assaults on free expression as the homicidal attack on the editors, staff, and cartoonists of *Charlie Hebdo* in Paris on January 7, 2015. The satirical weekly that held nothing sacred, not even Charles de Gaulle, exists within a French tradition of caustic satire, brazen caricature, and principled impertinence. It has waged a war of wits with the forces of militant Islam. Back in November 2011, the magazine had had the unmitigated gall of mocking sharia [in French *charia*], religious rule based on ancient Muslim principles unmodified by anything resembling a Reformation, an Enlightenment, or an Ecumenical Council. The cartoon on the cover of the issue entitled *Charia Hebdo* threatened "100 lashes if you don't die laughing!"[5] Five years earlier, the weekly reprinted the Danish cartoons of Mohammad that had aroused the ire of cutthroat jihadists. Surprisingly many publications in America and abroad did not have the guts to do so. The editors of *Charlie Hebdo*, including the legendary figures known as "Charb" (Stephane Charbonnier) and "Cabu" (Jean Cabut), were among the twelve individuals killed in the attack of January 7. For the right to say what they thought they paid with their lives.

On the very night that the Paris massacre dominated the news waves, with Parisians in the streets holding up signs saying "Je Suis Charlie," I heard a *New York Times* columnist go on CNN and tell newscaster Don Lemon that "We in journalism should try to avoid giving offense." It struck me as a very odd thing for him to say. Isn't giving offense, provoking discussion, stirring the pot, airing your views, part of the deal? A former press secretary to President Obama drew a distinction to the effect that while the press has the *right* to insult a religious leader, it may show bad *judgment* to wave a red flag in the eye of a stampeding bull. This is too halfhearted a defense of the freedom of speech and press, both of them under constant assault. In contrast, consider what "Charb" said, paraphrasing a line sometimes attributed to Emiliano Zapata, hero of the Mexican Revolution: "I'd rather die on my feet than live on my knees."

★ ★ ★

Sherman Alexie is writing the best poetry of his life. That is my opinion, but I am not alone in holding it. Sherman's work was chosen for the last four editions of *The Best American Poetry*: by Kevin Young (2011), Mark Doty (2012), Denise Duhamel (2013), and Terrance Hayes (2014), in addition to his inclusion in *The Best of the Best* retrospective volume that Robert Pinsky edited in 2013. Alexie mixes colloquial diction and formal virtuosity; he uses forms—a narrative sequence of numbered sentences, a prose sonnet, a ghazal—to restrain and paradoxically to accentuate the power of raw emotion that his poems deliver.

Sherman's reputation goes far beyond the precincts of verse. He

5. *"100 coups de fouet, si vous n'êtes pas morts de rire!"*

is celebrated for his fiction—*The Absolutely True Diary of a Part-Time Indian, The Lone Ranger and Tonto Fistfight in Heaven.* His prose has won him PEN prizes and a National Book Award. *Smoke Signals*, the movie he wrote, won accolades at the 1995 Sundance Festival. Just recently *Time* magazine rated *The Absolutely True Diary of a Part-Time Indian* as the "all-time" top young adult book above *Harry Potter, Charlotte's Web, The Phantom Tollbooth,* and Judy Blume.[6]

But poetry has a special place in Alexie's prolific portfolio. It can be said of Sherman that poetry saved his life. An alcoholic trying to recover control, he went off the wagon on March 11, 1991. He binged; he behaved badly. But it was the last time he has had a drink. The next day he went to the mailbox and found a letter from Dick Lourie of Hanging Loose Press accepting a manuscript of Alexie's poems for publication. "There was a sign," Sherman says.

Sherman undertook the task of editing this volume with great zest and he devoted himself tirelessly to scanning online journals, more of which are represented this year than ever before. In fact, more poems were chosen from the Academy of American Poets Poem-a-Day feature, skillfully edited by Alex Dimitrov, than from any other source. More magazines are represented altogether; fewer poems come from wide-circulation journals or expected places. The spirit of democracy on display is nevertheless not inconsistent with the search for literary excellence.

There are those who expect our "hyphenated" poets to write obsessively or even exclusively about their identity and to demonstrate a degree of social responsibility to the group they represent. But Sherman's poetry rebuffs this patronizing expectation. A Spokane/Coeur d'Alene tribal member, Sherman grew up on a reservation and he has, as a result, a fertile source of subject matter. But his aim is to write good poems, not to represent a tribe, and he brings to his writing the exemplary qualities of intelligence and humor. Jessica Chapel of *The Atlantic* remarked that Alexie's characters wonder "what it means to be an Indian, what they are told it means to be an Indian, and how to present themselves as Indians both to whites and other Indians." Then the reporter asked the author: "Is this struggle or uncertainty endemic to the American Indian experience?"

"It's endemic to everybody's experience," Alexie replied. "I think we're all struggling with our identity. Literature is all about the search

6. *Time*, January 19, 2015, p. 62.

for identity, regardless of the ethnicity. Southern, New Yorker, black, white, Asian, immigrant—everyone's trying to find a sense of belonging. In *The Toughest Indian*, the journalist's primary struggle is not ethnic identity, but his sexuality. I don't think he knows any of his identities. One of the points I was trying to make in that story is that being Indian is just part of who we are. I suppose the big difference in Indian literature is that Indians are indigenous to this country, so all non-Indian literature could be seen as immigrant literature. The search for immigrant identity is much different than the search for indigenous identity, so I suppose if you're indigenous to a place and you're still searching for your identity, that's pretty ironic."[7]

★ ★ ★

Mark Strand, who died on November 29, 2014, was the guest editor of the 1991 volume in this series. At the time we worked together, he had completed *The Continuous Life* and was writing *Dark Harbor*, two of his best books. I was finishing *Signs of the Times*, my book on deconstruction and Paul de Man, cheered by Mark's support—he loathed French critical theory and its effect on higher education. We would have long phone conversations twice a week or more to go over the poems that had come in and to talk about the shape of *The Best American Poetry 1991* as it evolved. We picked a Hopper for the cover; Mark was writing a book on him. As we went into production he wrote a beautiful introductory essay that I had no trouble placing with *The New York Times Book Review*, which ran it on its front page. The series was still young enough that it seemed to demand all the attention we could give it, and we gave readings at Seton Hall University in New Jersey and at various New York locales. And then there were always bookstores to visit (the Strand!) or a Neil Welliver opening to attend as our friendship grew.

Mark was a connoisseur of poems—as of so many things, from wine and food to clothes and paintings. His work would give off a casual, even effortless feel, as if the poet (who had initially studied to be a painter) were possessed of a certain kind of natural grace camouflaging all the craft and hard work. In *Dark Harbor*, he presents himself as a lucky man who knows the good life, striding on the pavement in his new dark blue double-breasted suit, lean and lanky, fresh after lunch at Lutèce with his longtime editor. The picture is accurate. He was a poet of unusual glamour (light is "the mascara of Eden") and of romance.

7 . *The Atlantic*, June 2000.

Yet the prevailing feeling in the depth of his best work is melancholy. If mortality is our first and last problem, the need to say farewell is continuous. Death is the mother of beauty; poetry is a valediction forbidding mourning. A man and a woman—in one of Strand's late prose poems ("Provisional Eternity")—lie in bed. The man keeps saying "Just one more time." The woman wonders why he keeps saying that. "Because I never want it to end," he says. And what is it that he doesn't want to end? "This never wanting it to end." Farewell, friend.

Sherman Alexie was born in 1966 and grew up in Wellpinit, Washington, on the Spokane Indian Reservation. His first collection of stories, *The Lone Ranger and Tonto Fistfight in Heaven* (1993), won a PEN/Hemingway Award. His first novel, *Reservation Blues*, received an American Book Award in 1996. In collaboration with Chris Eyre, a Cheyenne/Arapaho Indian filmmaker, Alexie adapted a story from that book, "This Is What it Means to Say Phoenix, Arizona," into the screenplay for the movie *Smoke Signals*, which won the Audience Award and Filmmakers Trophy at the 1998 Sundance Film Festival. *The Absolutely True Diary of a Part-Time Indian*, a semiautobiographical novel, appeared from Little, Brown Books for Children and won the 2007 National Book Award for Young People's Literature. His most recent books are the poetry collection *Face* from Hanging Loose Press, and *War Dances*, stories and poems from Grove Press, which was awarded the 2010 PEN/Faulkner Award for fiction. *Blasphemy*, a collection of new and selected stories, appeared in 2012 from Grove Press. He is lucky enough to be a full-time writer and lives with his family in Seattle.

INTRODUCTION

by Sherman Alexie

◊ ◊ ◊

In lieu of a conventional introduction, we present these statements by Sherman Alexie and conclude with a poem of his that appeared in the *Beloit Poetry Journal* in 2010:

"Poetry = Anger x Imagination."

"You know, people speak in poetry all the time. They just don't realize it."

"I write less about alcohol, less and less and less. You're an addict—so of course you write about the thing you love most. I loved alcohol the most, loved it more than anybody or anything. That's what I wrote about. And it certainly accounted for some great writing. But it accounted for two or three years of good writing—it would never account for twenty years of good writing. I would have turned into Charles Bukowski. He wrote 10,000 poems and 10 of them were great."

"They've been screaming about the death of literacy for years, but I think TV is the Gutenberg press. I think TV is the only thing that keeps us vaguely in democracy even if it's in the hands of the corporate culture. If you're an artist you write in your time. Moaning about the fact that maybe people read more books a hundred years ago—that's not true. I think the same percentage has always read."

[In reply to "What books might we be surprised to find on your shelves?"]: "The collected Harold Bloom!"

"I suppose, as an Indian living in the U.S., I'm used to crossing real and imaginary boundaries, and have, in fact, enjoyed a richer and crazier and more magical life precisely because I have fearlessly and fearfully crossed all sorts of those barriers. I guess I approach my poetry the same way I have approached every other thing in my life. I just don't like being told what to do. I write whatever feels and sounds right to me. At the beginning of my career, I wrote free verse with some formal influences, but I have lately been writing more formal verse with free verse influences. I don't feel the need to spend all my time living on either the free verse or the formal reservation. I want it all; hunger is my crime."

"My earliest interest in formalism came from individual poems rather than certain poets. Marvell's 'To His Coy Mistress,' Roethke's 'My Papa's Waltz,' Gwendolyn Brooks's 'We Real Cool,' and Langston Hughes's 'A Dream Deferred' are poems that come to mind as early formal poems I admired. Speaking both seriously and facetiously, I think I've spent my whole career rewriting 'My Papa's Waltz' with an Indian twist. Lately, as I've been writing much more formally—with end rhyme, a tenuous dance with meter, and explicit form—I've discovered that in writing toward that end rhyme, that accented or unaccented syllable, or that stanza break, I am constantly surprising myself with new ideas, new vocabulary, and new ways of looking at the world. The conscious use of form seems to have freed my subconscious."

"When you read a piece of writing that you admire, send a note of thanks to the author. Be effusive with your praise. Writing is a lonely business. Do your best to make it a little less lonely."

"I write poems naturally. I'm writing them all the time. I think it's more of a reflex talent than fiction is for me. Seems like I have to work harder to write fiction. That said, poems are much more demanding, you have fewer words, you can make fewer mistakes. You know, if you write a ten-line poem, you really can't make any mistakes. If you do, the poem is terrible. But when you write a novel, you have all that space to mess up in and people are more forgiving. So I think poetry audiences are far more demanding than fiction audiences are."

"Though I have a reputation for being a Luddite, I actually love the new digital technology and its artistic possibilities. So I have certainly been writing very short stories because they look great on my iPad screen! It's a callback to my early days of writing. I began my career on a manual typewriter and found that the physical act of pulling a sheet from the typewriter dictated the end of a poem. So I mostly wrote very short poems as a result. But when I moved to a word processor, my poems grew in length. And then I began to write stories and the beginnings of novels. The shape of the machine influences the shape of my work."

"Non-Indian writers usually say 'Great Spirit,' 'Mother Earth,' 'Two-Legged, Four-Legged, and Winged.' Mixed-blood writers usually say 'Creator,' 'Mother Earth,' 'Two-Legged, Four-Legged, and Winged.' Indian writers usually say 'God,' 'Mother Earth,' 'Human Being, Dog, and Bird.'"

"When I had no money, and a great book came out, I couldn't get it. I had to wait. I love the idea that I have hardcover books here and at home that I haven't read yet. That's how I view that I'm rich. I have hardcover books I may never read."

Defending Walt Whitman

Basketball is like this for young Indian boys, all arms and legs
and serious stomach muscles. Every body is brown!
These are the twentieth-century warriors who will never kill,
although a few sat quietly in the deserts of Kuwait,
waiting for orders to do something, to do something.

God, there is nothing as beautiful as a jumpshot
on a reservation summer basketball court
where the ball is moist with sweat,
and makes a sound when it swishes through the net
that causes Walt Whitman to weep because it is so perfect.

There are veterans of foreign wars here
although their bodies are still dominated
by collarbones and knees, although their bodies still respond
in the ways that bodies are supposed to respond when we are young.
Every body is brown! Look there, that boy can run
up and down this court forever. He can leap for a rebound

with his back arched like a salmon, all meat and bone
synchronized, magnetic, as if the court were a river,
as if the rim were a dam, as if the air were a ladder
leading the Indian boy toward home.

Some of the Indian boys still wear their military haircuts
while a few have let their hair grow back.
It will never be the same as it was before!
One Indian boy has never cut his hair, not once, and he braids it
into wild patterns that do not measure anything.
He is just a boy with too much time on his hands.
Look at him. He wants to play this game in bare feet.

God, the sun is so bright! There is no place like this.
Walt Whitman stretches his calf muscles
on the sidelines. He has the next game.
His huge beard is ridiculous on the reservation.
Some body throws a crazy pass and Walt Whitman catches it
with quick hands. He brings the ball close to his nose
and breathes in all of its smells: leather, brown skin, sweat,
black hair, burning oil, twisted ankle, long drink of warm water,
gunpowder, pine tree. Walt Whitman squeezes the ball tightly.
He wants to run. He hardly has the patience to wait for his turn.
"What's the score?" he asks. He asks, "What's the score?"

Basketball is like this for Walt Whitman. He watches these Indian boys
as if they were the last bodies on earth. Every body is brown!
Walt Whitman shakes because he believes in God.
Walt Whitman dreams of the Indian boy who will defend him,
trapping him in the corner, all flailing arms and legs
and legendary stomach muscles. Walt Whitman shakes
because he believes in God. Walt Whitman dreams
of the first jumpshot he will take, the ball arcing clumsily
from his fingers, striking the rim so hard that it sparks.
Walt Whitman shakes because he believes in God.
Walt Whitman closes his eyes. He is a small man and his beard
is ludicrous on the reservation, absolutely insane.
His beard makes the Indian boys righteously laugh. His beard
frightens the smallest Indian boys. His beard tickles the skin
of the Indian boys who dribble past him. His beard, his beard!

God, there is beauty in every body. Walt Whitman stands
at center court while the Indian boys run from basket to basket.
Walt Whitman cannot tell the difference between
offense and defense. He does not care if he touches the ball.
Half of the Indian boys wear t-shirts damp with sweat
and the other half are bareback, skin slick and shiny.
There is no place like this. Walt Whitman smiles.
Walt Whitman shakes. This game belongs to him.

THE
BEST
AMERICAN
POETRY
2015

Bodhisattva

◇   ◇   ◇

The new news is I love you my nudist
the new news is I love you my buddhist

my naked body and budding pleasure
in the weather of your presence

Not whether your presence but how
Oh love a new nodule of neurosis

a posy of new roses proposing
a new era for us *nobis pacem*

Oh my bodhisattva of new roses
you've saved me from my no-love neurosis

You've saved my old body from the fatwa
Let's lie down in a bed of roses

a pocketful that rings round the rosy
If this is the end of the world my love

let's fall down in bed and die
Let's give a new nod to nothing

Let's give a rosebud to nothing at all
How I love the new roses of nothing

Oh my bodhisattva of nothing
boding I hope no news but this

For our bodies and souls I hope nothing
but the weather of us in our peace

from Poem-a-Day

Cedars of Lebanon

◇   ◇   ◇

His legs are as pillars of marble, set upon sockets of fine gold:
his countenance is as Lebanon, excellent as the cedars.
—Song of Songs 5:15

If you can see them, the snow-covered
cedars, crowning the hills, come

to the cabin between the two tallest,
their branches hooked

with the tantrums of crows.

~~

Will you find me without the pink and blue hydrangeas?

Will you find me without the spikes of St. Augustine grass?

Will you find me with the bloodied snow—where some frail thing was

raptured?

~~

If you find a stag and kill it,

throw its hind legs over your shoulder
and drag it to my cabin
between the tallest cedars.

Its blood on the snow is my voice pursuing you.

~~

I sleep on a cedar bed
with red fur blankets,

the wood of the gates of paradise,
wood which hid the naked couple.

Wood of shame. Wood of passage.

If you come, I'll press my hand
to your chest. A key

to the fittings of a lock.

~~

You knock at the door.
Break several cedar branches

and dust off the snow.
Bring in seven for the bedroom,

seven for the fireplace,
then rest your head on my chest—

even bare
branches can make a kind of summer.

from *Burrow Press Review*

A Retrograde

◇ ◇ ◇

She crept into my room, took me outside into the mosquito night thick with the gutted hums of fishermen's wives, piercing the flesh of a sleepwalking sky.

She taught me that cobwebs are hammocks for spirits, a stop along the way to rest their weary skins, a knot on the thread of their pilgrimage to a place they had almost touched once.

In those days, a village could grow legs. Wedge itself deep into the throat of mountains where horses couldn't smell it, where footsteps couldn't sear its memory onto peeling roads.

Dear mama: The orchids have teeth
the machetes are ornaments
rusting upon the walls.

I want to build you a temple
of teeth
but my hands are too tender
my hands are for stringing
the rice grains of rosaries.

Dear mama: On the ocean roams a shadow of splinters
the fish are hurling themselves onto the shore
the shore will break into birds of dust
the scales are mirrors
blinding the sun.

On the ocean roams a shadow of splinters
how will I swim to you
when the day is done?

from *Muzzle*

WFM: Allergic to Pine-Sol, Am I the Only One

◊　◊　◊

—lines from Craigslist personal ads

Hi. I react really badly to Pine-Sol. My eyelids swell up and my eyes
turn bright red. I am a REAL woman. It is January 1, 2014.
Educated men move to the top of the list.
We were both getting gas Wednesday evening. Fish counter, Giant Eagle:
My husband knows how attractive I find you.
You caught me singing loudly. Your name means "wind."
This Christmas season marks my eighth year of being single.
Please have a car (truck preferably) and a job.
I collect candles and have two grown children who are on their own now
thank God. I already bought your birthday present—
It's a tie. With swordfish on it. There are certain things
my nose can't handle and smoking is one of them.
I signed up to volunteer at a local park for a Merry not Scary
trick or treat trail—it would be nice to have a companion.
Must be willing to be seen in public with a size 16 woman.
I'm a little bigger, but not sloppy-fat. Six one four five nine eight
two three one nine. I can swing a hammer and am a pro
at putting on makeup. Sexiness to me is you
plus a photographic memory. Do you have questions
you've always wanted to ask a woman? You left your receipt
and that's how I figured out your name. I was behind you
at the Lane Avenue Starbucks drive thru and you paid
for my grande nonfat no whip Mocha Frapp.
Your silver hair was gorgeous. Wow. The first time
we made love our souls connected and intertwined

and seemed to remember they were destined for one another. Let's go to the shooting range. I have no business expertise, but I'd love a guy who is good with rope.

from *The Journal*

Swallowed

◇   ◇   ◇

When I see an escalator I have to kiss
everyone on it, don't you? If you like these

pastries—our lawyer calls them perfidy rolls—
there are more on his helicopter.

He's Serbian or something,
whole family wiped out

by his other family. But he's fine now.
Drop a kiss on the cultural floor,

three-second rule applies. I don't even know
who I'm kissing anymore, do you?

Sneak away to where the world snaps in half
and come back with sanctions, come back

with sauces, come back with Haribo,
come back with *Inferno* flashcards,

come back with the glottal nonstop.
Dear Ciacco, your flowers were delicious but barely

a lunch so we dug a new grave for the stems.
"Finish us up," they sang, "or finish us off."

Lie down in sewage to stay down; sit up
only for people-will-see-me-and-die-level fame,

smiling like your teeth are on fire.
Oh darling you know what they say:

why have one factory
when you can have five. Our lawyer always

reminds us, "Little hands, long hours." Indeed!
If I could eat my voice I would, but I'm off

to seize the world, the inside of its machine.
This is the way Celan ends, not with a bang

but a river. Woolf, too; she goes out
the same goddamn way—

I mean, wind any creature tight
enough and it does what it has to do.

from *Lemon Hound*

A Scatology

◇   ◇   ◇

Abracadabra: The anus. The star at the base of the human
balloon. Close it tight as the sun, then let it unfurl:
Crepe paper, the spiraling heart of the pipecleaner flower.

Do you know what to do? Pry open that shopworn diary.
Easy. Use your fingertips, mirrors. See what you're hiding
from yourself. Use spoons to reflect: Your ass, backwards,
goes raveling outward like an expanding universe.

Have you considered *muscerdae*, the soft and smooth
innumerable droppings of mice? *Guano*, the bats' own
jellicate wallpaper? Read those fewtrils for alphabets and become
kahuna. Revere their secret dictations until,

like all things, the secrets reorder the order of your language.
Make those soft, inward labyrinths your own. Know them
not for their oubliettes alone, but for what they release:
Omina. Fortuna. The ways in which you see and might become.

Parousia. That moment in which the body feels least heavy, most
quiet, uncalmably calm. Consider: Between *scatology* and *eschatology*
remains only "he." Not "the man" or "man" or "men" but Old English,
see? Us all, perhaps, though this is not the point. The point is

this: We can take in language from either end and make language
understood—again, from either end. Embrace your exits, where bloom
virginities of every orifice. Where bloom oracles: We are all full of shit.

We could choose to make this space in us so small no digit, no wind, no
x could ever pass through. Or we could open a world any finger or tongue
(yours?) could enter into and speak. We could make a primer. Have you considered:

Zero—the shape that comes to mind—in its most common, most practical functions
    makes everything the same as or equal to itself.

from *Ninth Letter*

CHANA BLOCH

The Joins

◊ ◊ ◊

*Kintsugi is the Japanese art of mending
precious pottery with gold.*

What's between us
seems flexible as the webbing
between forefinger and thumb.

Seems flexible but isn't;
what's between us
is made of clay

like any cup on the shelf.
It shatters easily. Repair
becomes the task.

We glue the wounded edges
with tentative fingers.
Scar tissue is visible history

and the cup is precious to us
because
we saved it.

In the art of *kintsugi*
a potter repairing a broken cup
would sprinkle the resin

with powdered gold.
Sometimes the joins
are so exquisite

they say the potter
may have broken the cup
just so he could mend it.

from *The Southern Review* and *Poetry Daily*

House Is an Enigma

◊　◊　◊

House is not a metaphor. House has nothing
to do with beak or wing. House is not two

hands held angled towards each other. House is
not its roof or the pine straw on its roof. At night,

its windows and doors look nothing like a face.
Its stairs are not vertebrae. Its walls may be

white. They are not pale skin. House does not
appreciate your pun on its panes as pains.

House does not appreciate because house
does not have feelings. House has no aesthetic

program. House does what it does, which is
not doing. House does not sit on its foundations.

House exists in its foundations, and when the wind
pushes itself to full gale, house is never the one crying.

from *Conduit*

Prayer at 3 a.m.

◊   ◊   ◊

I washed your father's pants in the kitchen sink.
That should have been enough to tell you.
I am still convinced there is no difference
between kneeling and falling if you don't get up.

The head goes down in defeat, but lower in prayer,
and your sister tells me each visit that she has learned
of a new use for her hands.

I've seen this from you both: cartwheels through the field
at dawn, toes popping above the corn stalks like fleas
over the heads of lepers. Your scarecrow reminds me

of Jesus, his guilt confused for fear.
The sun doesn't know; the fog lifts
everything in praise.

from *The Volta*

Makeshift

◊　◊　◊

From two pieces of string and oil-fattened feathers he made a father.
She made a mother from loss buttons and ocean debris.

Lacking a grave, they embottled themselves
in a favorite liqueur, the pyx and plethora of clouds—

with the heart striped and clear-cut, they rekindled the stars,
created a glossary of seeds.

Down the fire ladder, rung after fiery rung, they gather, salvage,
fiddle about, curse and root, laugh themselves silly,

en masse assemble a makeshift holy city. In the holy city,
makeshift, they assemble en masse, silly themselves,

laugh and root, curse the fiddle, gather salvage rung
after fiery rung as they ladder their fire down.

A glossary seeded creates stars, strips clear the diamond-cut heart.

They sold clouds, the plethora and pyx of liqueur. Favored themselves
embottled in grave lack, ocean debris, and loss buttons,

where Mother made a father who made feathers
from fattened oil and string pieces for two.

from *The New Yorker*

in the hall of the ruby-throated warbler

◇   ◇   ◇

Jenny, sunny Jenny, beige-honey Jenny
sings the parsley up from the topsoil, Jenny,
cool tabouleh, hot apple crumble Jenny,
alchemy Jenny

please, I whispered, *teach me the secret whistle*
help me coax the thistledown from the thistle
perch me on the branch where the goldfinch rustles
heedless of bristles

so she bore my heart to the eagle's aerie
folded me like down in a twig-tight nestle
kissed me til my sinews leapt up, cat's cradle
brain like a beehive

Jenny, downy Jenny, my treetop lover

from *Able Muse*

Homeland

◇ ◇ ◇

I knew I had jet lag because no one would make love to me.
All the men thought me a vampire. All the women were

Women. In America that year, black people kept dreaming
That the president got shot. Then the president got shot

Breaking into the White House. He claimed to have lost
His keys. What's the proper name for a man caught stealing

Into his own home? I asked a few passengers. They replied,
Jigger. After that, I took the red-eye. I took to a sigh deep

As the end of a day in the dark fields below us. Some slept,
But nobody named Security ever believes me. Confiscated—

My Atripla. My Celexa. My Cortisone. My Klonopin. My
Flexeril. My Zyrtec. My Nasarel. My Percocet. My Ambien.

Nobody in this nation feels safe, and I'm still a reason why.
Every day, something gets thrown away on account of long

History or hair or fingernails or, yes, of course, my fangs.

from *Fence*

RAFAEL CAMPO

"DOCTORS LIE, MAY HIDE MISTAKES"

◇   ◇   ◇

—Boston Globe *headline*

That doctors lie, may hide mistakes
should come as no surprise. Of course
the body we must memorize
in fact cannot be trusted, breasts
embarrassing as cheese soufflés
that didn't rise, scuffed knees as dumb
as grief. The very act of touch
is like a lie, the latex gloves
we wear in case of a mistake
protecting us from pulsing blood's
blithe truths. We lie and hide from what
the stethoscope will try to say,
incapable of listening
itself: the heart, mistaken for
the place where the elusive soul
resides, in fact does not repeat
itself. Instead, it cries, "Of course
we must tell lies, and to be human
is this incalculable mistake."

from *upstreet*

JULIE CARR

A fourteen-line poem on sex

◊ ◊ ◊

1. On film I'm a sky or a swimmer

2. Red lightbulb

3. All those cross-legged girls

4. If I don't write the word "rendered"

5. I will forget it by morning

6. Boys in black sing harmonies

7. She's running a fever dressed like a Belgian

8. Can you smell her from here?

9. A mutating ghost

10. Once on a drive from Nashville to Asheville

11. I ran out of gas. I'd been watching the temperature gauge

12. Resolutely in the middle

13. I'd never run out of gas before

14. I didn't know what was wrong with the car

from *The Kenyon Review*

for i will do/undo what was done/undone to me

◊　◊　◊

i pledge allegiance to the already fallen snow
& to the snow now falling. to the old snow & the new.
to foot & paw & tire prints in the snow both young & aging,
the deep & shallow marks left on cold streets, our long

misbegotten manuscripts. i pledge allegiance to the weather
report that promises more snow, plus freezing rain.
though i would minus the pluvial & plus the multitude

of messages pressed muddy into the perfectly
mutable snow, i have faith in the report that goes on to read:
by the end of the week, there will be an increased storm-related
illegibility of the asphalt & concrete & brick. for i pledge

betrayal to the fantasy of ever reading anything
completely. for i will do/undo what was done/undone to me:
to be brought into a patterned world of weathers

& reports. & thus i pledge allegiance to the always
partial, the always translated, the always never
of knowing who's walking around, what's being left behind,
the signs, the cries, the breadcrumbs & the blood. the toe-

nails & armpit hair of our trying & failing to speak
our specks of *here* to the *everywhere*. dirty snow of my weary
city, i ask you to tell me a story about your life

& you tell me you've left for another country,
but forgot your suitcase. at the airport they told you
not to worry, all your things have already been sent
to your new place by your ninth grade french teacher,

the only nice one. & the weather where your true love is
is governed by principles or persons you can't name,

imagine. it is that good, or bad.

from *PANK*

Careful, I Just Won a Prize at the Fair

◊ ◊ ◊

Don't remind me
how insufficient
love is. You

threw quarters
into a bowl. We are bones
and need, all hair

and want: this fish won't swim
in a plastic bag
forever. My makeshift

gown is a candle, my breasts
full of milk for our young—
whose flames

are these anyway?

from *Columbia Poetry Review*

The Bees, the Flowers, Jesus, Ancient Tigers, Poseidon, Adam and Eve

◊ ◊ ◊

Huh! That bumblebee looks ridiculous staggering its way

across those blue flowers, the ones I can never
remember the name of. Do you know the old engineer's

joke: that, theoretically, bees can't fly? But they look so

perfect together, like Absolute Purpose incarnate: one bee
plus one blue flower equals about a billion

years of symbiosis. Which leads me to wonder what it is

I'm doing here, peering through a lens at the thigh-pouches
stuffed with pollen and the baffling intricacies

of stamen and pistil. Am I supposed to say something, add
a soundtrack and voiceover? My life's spent

running an inept tour for my own sad swindle of a vacation

until every goddamned thing's reduced to botched captions
and dabs of misinformation in fractured,

not-quite-right English: *Here sir, that's the very place Jesus*

wept. The Colosseum sprouts and blooms with leftover seeds
pooped by ancient tigers. Poseidon diddled

Philomel in the warm slap of this ankle-deep surf to the dying
stings of a thousand jellyfish. There, probably,

atop yonder scraggly hillock, Adam should've said no to Eve.

from *Prairie Schooner*

ERICA DAWSON

Slow-Wave Sleep with a Fairy Tale

◇   ◇   ◇

I knocked out Sleeping Beauty, fucking cocked
her on the jaw. She fell into the briar.
Pussy. I found her prince. I up and socked
him, too. I called each one of them a liar.

I damned the spindle's hundred years of sleep
because I rarely sleep. I cursed the birds
who took their heads from out beneath their heap
of wings. When lovers look, they need no words.

And when a hound came running after me,
a Redbone with a smile bearing its teeth
so white, I woke up with the majesty
of a princess who's lying underneath

a spell of something better still to come.
My eyes were blurry, my mouth dry and dumb.

from *Tupelo Quarterly*

DANIELLE DeTIBERUS

In a Black Tank Top

◊ ◊ ◊

In a black tank top
my man can say
just about anything.
Stuff like, *let's watch*
football, or *this shrimp*
is overcooked or *see how many pull-ups I*
can do. In a black tank top, he looks fifteen
years younger, looks like all those silly boys
I knew in school. When he gets home from
playing ball, I want to crawl inside the bed
of his parents' beat-up red pick-up truck &
make out until his almost beard scratches
at me, leaves dappled marks on my cheeks
& throat for friends to stare at for days. In a
black tank top, I can watch him talk about
beams, joists, & trusses for hours cause the
shadows of his arm press against the ribbed
cotton like a boy presses a girl up against a
steely locker, hard before Mrs. Toner's home
room. I want to shout, *Damn son! Looking*
like that should be illegal. And, *Break me off*
some of that. Instead I try to be the shy little
thing, smile & blush like the good girls do. In
a black tank top, though, my man always gets
me to offer a hand to pull it off. He trembles:
a   boy   undoing   his   first   real   belt.

from *Rattle*

It Was the Animals

◇   ◇   ◇

Today my brother brought over a piece of the ark
wrapped in a white plastic grocery bag.

He set the bag on my dining table, unknotted it,
peeled it away, revealing a foot-long fracture of wood.
He took a step back and gestured toward it
with his arms and open palms—

> *It's the ark*, he said.
> *You mean Noah's ark?* I asked.
> *What other ark is there?* he answered.

> *Read the inscription*, he told me,
> *it tells what's going to happen at the end.*
> *What end?* I wanted to know.
> He laughed, *What do you mean, "what end"?*
> *The end end.*

Then he lifted it out. The plastic bag rattled.
His fingers were silkened by pipe blisters.
He held the jagged piece of wood so gently.
I had forgotten my brother could be gentle.

He set it on the table the way people on television
set things when they're afraid those things might blow up
or go off—he set it right next to my empty coffee cup.

It was no ark—
it was the broken end of a picture frame
with a floral design carved into its surface.

He put his head in his hands—

>   *I shouldn't show you this—*
>   *God, why did I show her this?*
>   *It's ancient—O, God,*
>   *this is so old.*

>   *Fine*, I gave in, *Where did you get it?*
>   *The girl*, he said. *O, the girl.*
>   *What girl?* I asked.
>   *You'll wish you never knew*, he told me.

I watched him drag his wrecked fingers
over the chipped flower-work of the wood—

>   *You should read it. But, O, you can't take it—*
>   *no matter how many books you've read.*

He was wrong. I could take the ark.
I could even take his marvelously fucked fingers.
The way they almost glittered.

It was the animals—the animals I could not take—

they came up the walkway into my house,
cracked the doorframe with their hooves and hips,
marched past me, into my kitchen, into my brother,

tails snaking across my feet before disappearing
like retracting vacuum cords into the hollows
of my brother's clavicles, tusks scraping the walls,

reaching out for him—wildebeests, pigs,
the oryxes with their black matching horns,
javelinas, jaguars, pumas, raptors. The ocelots

with their mathematical faces. So many kinds of goat.
So many kinds of creature.

I wanted to follow them, to get to the bottom of it,
but my brother stopped me—

> *This is serious*, he said.
> *You have to understand.*
> *It can save you.*

So I sat down, with my brother wrecked open like that,
and two-by-two the fantastical beasts
parading him. I sat, as the water fell against my ankles,
built itself up around me, filled my coffee cup
before floating it away from the table.

My brother—teeming with shadows—
a hull of bones, lit only by tooth and tusk,
lifting his ark high in the air.

from *Poetry*

Fornicating

◊　◊　◊

> such a beautiful
> day
> and I'm not
> fornicating
>
> —Adília Lopes

I have goose bumps
from the breeze
coming into the window
which is a kind of fornication
but who am I kidding
a breeze is not even a kiss
especially a breeze
strained through a screen

I would have a better chance
out on the street
where I could perhaps meet
someone who wanted
to fornicate
with me or someone like me
and I could pretend
I suppose
even to be someone else
give a fake name
so the man would never
find me again

it is a little scary to say
to a stranger, *Hey, do you*
want to fornicate?
especially if you are a woman
and you want to fornicate
with a man

what kind of a man
would say yes to such a request

maybe a violent one
maybe no decent man at all
since the request is pretty bold
and I suppose I would
look crazy

men are leery of crazy women
and I can't blame them

I could promise a man
that I wouldn't
stalk him or call him ever
that I am just in it
for the fornication
but would he believe me

even I don't really believe me

because what if the fornication
was a success and I woke up
the next morning
another beautiful day
and I wasn't satisfied
with just the memory
of fornication
and wanted another round

or what if it was lousy
outside
and since I'd given a fake name

insisting I didn't want to know his
I had to look for a new fornicator
this time while lugging an umbrella

this time I could look for a woman
with the same sad look I have
when I want to fornicate
and if she agreed
we could step out of the rain
into her apartment
it might not be as scary
as approaching another man
or as big a leap over a puddle

Anne Sexton wrote
Once I was beautiful. Now I am myself . . .
then Adília Lopes wrote
once I was beautiful now I'm myself
then I wrote
fornication is for all the beautiful
and unbeautiful selves
on both beautiful
and unbeautiful days

not that I knew what I meant
it's just that sometimes
it's easy to feel unbeautiful
when you have unmet desires
or embarrassed that you have
such desires at all

I once wrote about a lover
who would pet his cat
more than me
and my friend said
this poem is too vulnerable
I feel as though I should throw a coat
over this poem

she was right of course
and I tore it up
I only remember it today
because in her author's photo
Adília Lopes holds a cat

I am allergic to cats
the lover had to wash his hands
those many years ago
before he could touch me

Kurt Vonnegut wrote
that every character needs
to want something
even if that something
is only a glass of water

I want to fornicate

I get up from my chair
and press my face against
the cool screen
until there is a dirty grid on my cheek
as though I've slept

in fifty tiny beds

from *The Literary Review*

Vernacular Owl

◊   ◊   ◊

for Amiri Baraka

Old Ark,
how funky it was, all those animals, two of every kind,
and all that waste, the human shit somebody had to clean up.
Somebody, some love you hugged before fear,
the fear of an in-sani-nation, the No Blues, ruined your bowels.
Go devil.
Public programs
like
Race.
Dems a Repub
of dumpster molesters,
Congressional
whole-part bidders on your ugliest clown.
Left wing, right,
the missing moderates
of flightless fight.
Private
like
the Runs.
God evil.
Somebody had to clean that shit up.
Somebody, some love who raised you, wise.
Feathered razors for eyebrows,
alto,
tenor.

Wasn't no branch.
Some
say
a tree,
not
for rest either.
For change.

    When was we a wild life,
                    long-eared
                and short. Prey,
                some prayed for
            the flood. And were
                    struck by floating,
                corporate quintets
            of Rocks and Roths,
            assets bond Prestige.

First
Organizer
ever
called a
Nigga,
        Noah,
but not
the last
Occupier of Ararat
. . . got thick
on
Genesis
and electric cello, cell phone shaped UFOs
fueled by
the damp, murdered clay
of divinity-based
Racial
Mountain
Dirt.
        Somebody had to clean that shit up.

Some native body,
beside the smooth water,
 like a
brook

       Gwen say,
"I had to kick their law into their teeth in order to save them."

                           Chaser if
                           you straight.

Ark Old
Ark New
Ark Now

Only	Only
Sidney P	Simple JessB
would	would
___ Spencer T	___ Dizzy G
to turn	to accent
the dinner	the p's
cheek	not the ". . . nuts."

Change the record, Record Changer.
Name
Change
the changing same.

                   Something only you could Art Messenger
  & dig in any chord.
High water, like the woods of secrecy,
always a trail a ways a coming.
God evil.
Move the "d."
Go devil.
  The Mosque watchers know.
Also de wind, de wind
and de Word, spoken and written,
in hidden   in love
with the intestines

of Testament.
   Eyes like
  a woman's fist,
her hard facts—not the crying,
domestic consonants
   "of non being."
Soprano,
piano,
or the cultural cowardice
    of class,
in any chord
of standardized "sheeit" music, lowcoup risks slit.
   Though flawed, too,
by penetrable flesh,
some blue kind.
   Unlike
a pretty shield,
loaded free.

Wasn't just Winter
or lonely. Those.
Wasn't just Sundays
the living did not return.

   Crouch if you a bum or one of Mumbo Jumbo's reckless,
poisonous reeds. A neck crow man ser vant *n*
   a jes' grew suit.
Us am,
an unfit
second
Constitution.
   Us am, an ambulance full of . . .
broke-down,
as round as we bald.
   Obeying
hawkish
eagles.

   Why the young Brothers so big, what they eatin',
why they blow up like that, gotta wear big white tees, gotta wear white

skin sheets, like maggots, like lard, like they the domestic oil of death
and klan sweat, "who . . ." blew them up, doctored, "who . . ." pickin'
them off like dark cotton, make them make themselves a fashion of
profitable, soft muscular bales, somebody got to clean this shit up.

   All us, U.S. animals,
on one floating stage
we knew
was a toilet,
the third oldest in the nation, unreserved.
Wasn't no bank
or branch.
   Yes we Vatican, despite Alighieri's medium rare, rate of interest.
It
was
confirmation.
   Some say
black fire
wood.
  Some love that changed our screaming
  Atlantic bottoms
when all we
   could be
was thin olive sticks,
with battered whore-ti-cultural beaks, and eastern screech.

      Flushed, too, every time *The Yew Norker*
or one of Obi Wan Kenobi's traitorous X Jedi Clampett hillbillies
fresh prince'd us . . .

        The real religion,
        our "individual expressiveness"
           wasn't dehuman-u-factured
        by a Greek HAARP
              in a Roman uni-dot-gov-versity.

        Where we Away
        our Steel, "flood"
           means "flow."
        Where we Tenure

                    our Ammo, "podium"
                    means "drum."

Flood,
flow.
Podium,
drum.
Flood,
drum.
Podium,
flow.
Drum,
podium.
Flood,
flow.

    Used to be a whole lot of chalk around the Ark,
then anger, then angels, rehabbed wings made of fried white dust,
fallen from when the board of knowledge was public and named
after a stranger or [rich] crook, an anti-in immigrant-can'tameter
stretched across the teepee-skin, chairs of class

                    where we clapped
                the erasers,
                    fifty snows old,
                like we were
                the first Abraham,
                    where we clapped
                the Race Erasers
                and drove away
                    from K James V and K Leo PB
                in shiny Lincolns,
                sprinkling holy sheeple from the sky,
                their
                powdery
                absolute
                    Rule.
                Just add oil-water.
                Belongs
                to humanity.

                    ———
                     41

Just add sugar-rubber.
Belongs
to civilization.
Gold.
Days.
Nights.
Ounces.
A forty.
Mules move.
A forty.
Move.
Move.
Move
mule.

Whatyoumaycall "how we here" and get no
response . . . how we . . . where we fear, how we hear how we sound and
how sometimes [time is some] even our own sound fears us, faults us,
and remembers the first us, confronting Columbus with thunderbolts,
when "was-we" not good-citizen sober, "was-we" voting and drowning,
and rotting like "we-was" the wrong targets of the armed guts of our
own young?

Now a daze,
tribe-be-known,
the devil
the best historian we got.
Anyhow.

from *Poetry*

In Memory of My Parents Who Are Not Dead Yet

◊   ◊   ◊

Is it harder for the bachelorette or her suitors?

The brown oyster mushroom

on her face is possibly the most perfect

nose I have ever seen. I think people

might actually win love. The funny guy always

appeared safe but later you saw him

in the dark green yard

puking, a thin

sweat on the back of his neck.

I want the air I breathe

to maintain my body's

mystery. I worry I'll run into you at a party

then I remember I don't go to parties

so I'm safe. I have no godly discipline.

When someone yells I still huddle

under a want for ice cream.

How can you love people

without them feeling accused?

If I wanted to win

I would draw harder lines

and sit next to them, stay

awake, rattle the box of bullets.

When we touch my heart

gets green

and white, preppy, bordered,

oh! she says and perks up.

It hurts to not be everyone else. If love dies

it was already dead.

from *Powder Keg*

JAMES GALVIN

On the Sadness
of Wedding Dresses

◇   ◇   ◇

On starless, windless nights like this
I imagine
I can hear the wedding dresses
Weeping in their closets,
Luminescent with hopeless longing,
Like hollow angels.
They know they will never be worn again.
Who wants them now,
After their one heroic day in the limelight?
Yet they glow with desire
In the darkness of closets.
A few lucky wedding dresses
Get worn by daughters—just once more,
Then back to the closet.
Most turn yellow over time,
Yellow from praying
For the moths to come
And carry them into the sky.
Where is your mother's wedding dress,
What closet?
Where is your grandmother's wedding dress?
What, gone?
Eventually they all disappear,
Who knows where.
Imagine a dump with a wedding dress on it.
I saw one wedding dress, hopeful at Goodwill.

But what sad story brought it there,
And what sad story will take it away?
Somewhere a closet is waiting for it.
The luckiest wedding dresses
Are those of wives
Betrayed by their husbands
A week after the wedding.
They are flung outside the doublewide,
Or the condo in Telluride,
And doused with gasoline.
They ride the candolescent flames,
Just smoke now,
Into a sky full of congratulations.

from *The Iowa Review*

The Garden in August

◇   ◇   ◇

1.

Afternoon brings my neighbor outside
in her florid pink nightgown,
exposed breasts like pendulums

as she kneels in the gravel
speaking to an empty planter. As the two of us
wait in the kitchen

for her children, it is clear
her thoughts float
from the back of the skull to the front.

Unstoppered bottles. Pills on the table:

blood pressure cholesterol diabetes arrhythmic heart

dispensed out of sequence
from the calendar of forgotten days.

2.

How resigned she seems
to the eviction notices her body is receiving,

the way a daughter sags against
the door jamb.

Family members speak in code
about selling the house.

3.

Because she is a system of bone and blood

Because her hands are rusted hinges

Because wisps of spiderwebs float behind eyelids

Because her heart leaks and something has palmed a piece of one lung

Because her body is a test tube

4.

Tomorrow she will be outside again, offering
up her sweat to the sun

as she tends the perennials and
sluices water, working her garden

which is purpose, which is happiness—
even as petal and pistil we fall.

from *PMS: poemmemoirstory*

AMY GERSTLER

Rhinencephalon

◊　◊　◊

Your belly smells disheveled.
Your armpits smell like kelp.
Your genitals smell like lily flower soup
(no MSG, please). You claim weedy
scents of medicinal broth simmering
for sick infants emanate from my neck,
and that my recently doffed sox
smell of nothing but lust. Could we
sniff each other out, I wonder,
blindfolded, from among the massed souls
queuing up for free stew,
or being shoved into box cars,
or crouched under desks protecting
our necks in disaster drills,
or getting processed in tents at the edge
of a refugee camp? Do we really want
to pledge to enter heaven together
and to live on there forever
if heaven's bereft of smell?

from *The American Poetry Review*

A Sharply Worded Silence

◇ ◇ ◇

Let me tell you something, said the old woman.
We were sitting, facing each other,
in the park at _____, a city famous for its wooden toys.

At the time, I had run away from a sad love affair,
and as a kind of penance or self-punishment, I was working
at a factory, carving by hand the tiny hands and feet.

The park was my consolation, particularly in the quiet hours
after sunset, when it was often abandoned.
But on this evening, when I entered what was called the Contessa's Garden,
I saw that someone had preceded me. It strikes me now
I could have gone ahead, but I had been
set on this destination; all day I had been thinking of the cherry trees
with which the glade was planted, whose time of blossoming had nearly ended.

We sat in silence. Dusk was falling,
and with it came a feeling of enclosure
as in a train cabin.

When I was young, she said, I liked walking the garden path at twilight
and if the path was long enough I would see the moon rise.
That was for me the great pleasure: not sex, not food, not worldly amusement.
I preferred the moon's rising, and sometimes I would hear,
at the same moment, the sublime notes of the final ensemble
of *The Marriage of Figaro*. Where did the music come from?
I never knew.

Because it is the nature of garden paths
to be circular, each night, after my wanderings,
I would find myself at my front door, staring at it,
barely able to make out, in darkness, the glittering knob.

It was, she said, a great discovery, albeit my real life.

But certain nights, she said, the moon was barely visible through the clouds
and the music never started. A night of pure discouragement.
And still the next night I would begin again, and often all would be well.

I could think of nothing to say. This story, so pointless as I write it out,
was in fact interrupted at every stage with trance-like pauses
and prolonged intermissions, so that by this time night had started.

Ah the capacious night, the night
so eager to accommodate strange perceptions. I felt that some important secret
was about to be entrusted to me, as a torch is passed
from one hand to another in a relay.

My sincere apologies, she said.
I had mistaken you for one of my friends.
And she gestured toward the statues we sat among,
heroic men, self-sacrificing saintly women
holding granite babies to their breasts.
Not changeable, she said, like human beings.

I gave up on them, she said.
But I never lost my taste for circular voyages.
Correct me if I'm wrong.

Above our heads, the cherry blossoms had begun
to loosen in the night sky, or maybe the stars were drifting,
drifting and falling apart, and where they landed
new worlds would form.

Soon afterward I returned to my native city
and was reunited with my former lover.
And yet increasingly my mind returned to this incident,
studying it from all perspectives, each year more intensely convinced,

despite the absence of evidence, that it contained some secret.
I concluded finally that whatever message there might have been
was not contained in speech—so, I realized, my mother used to speak to me,
her sharply worded silences cautioning me and chastising me—

and it seemed to me I had not only returned to my lover
but was now returning to the Contessa's Garden
in which the cherry trees were still blooming
like a pilgrim seeking expiation and forgiveness,

so I assumed there would be, at some point,
a door with a glittering knob,
but when this would happen and where I had no idea.

from *The Threepenny Review*

R. S. GWYNN

Looney Tunes

◊   ◊   ◊

for John Whitworth

It begins with the division of a solitary cell,
Carcinogenetic fission leading to a passing-bell,
Lurking far beneath your vision like a pebble in a well—
       Then it grows.
Soon enough there comes a scalpel that is keen to save your life,
Crooning, "All things will be well, pal, if you just survive the knife,
But to climb the tallest Alp'll be much easier. Call your wife."
       Then it grows, grows, grows. Then it grows.

Say you can't remember Monday night when Tuesday rolls around.
Does it mean they'll find you one day blind and frothing on the ground?
Is it ominous that Sunday sermons make your temples pound?
       (How it shows!)
You may take the pledge, abstaining, thinking you can lick it all.
But it's hard when, ascertaining how diversions may enthrall,
You're still standing there and draining one well past the final call:
       How it shows, shows, shows. (How it shows!)

You may lose a set of car keys and mislay a name or face.
Does your mind demand bright marquees where each star must have its place?
It's like diving in the dark. It's less a river than a race.
       And it flows
Like the coming days of drivel, like the dreaded days of drool
When the very best you give'll prove you're just an antique fool,
And your thoughts will be so trivial as to lead to ridicule—
       And it flows, flows, flows. And it flows.

Do you want to be a burden? Can you stand to be a drag?
Make your mind up, say the word and do not let the moment lag.
When you go to get your guerdon let them see your battle flag!
        So it goes.
There'll be many there who'll miss you and a few to lend a hand,
There'll be boxes full of tissue, lots of awful music, and
Lissome maidens who won't kiss you as you seek the promised land.
        So it goes, goes, goes. So it goes.

        from *Able Muse*

Thumbs

◇ ◇ ◇

Tuck a severed thumb into a paper towel
and place it in a plastic bag on the window sill
to sprout a new one. Hydroponic tomatoes
don't taste as good as the ones on a vine.
It's a completely controlled environment
that has nothing to do with authenticity.
He made me a promise at our shotgun wedding.
He would take my thumbs if I ever slept
with another man. If you're on the train
to Cleveland, it's okay to get off at a whistle stop
but if you don't have a ticket, you have to say so.
Just say what you mean. I couldn't say I didn't love him.
In the little flash of a threat when you know you're going
to get hurt, you have to live up to it one way or another.
It's about listening, but the ear is one of the weakest
muscles in the body. Ten years after the promise
I slit my hand open on a bottle of wine over steak
with a man I thought I could love. The female cuckoo bird
does not settle down with a mate. Now we make her
come out of a clock. I sound like a local
when I give directions. I'm getting the hang of it.
If you have no ticket, say it. It's about knowing
where you want to put the stone in the wall.
You might need to cut that up for me,
since I have no thumbs. When he met the next man
I could love, he mentioned the promise.
It's difficult to go back to the land of the paved road.
Once the thumb-sprouts root, plant them.

When they sex themselves, you have to split them
so they don't contaminate each other.

from *The Southampton Review*

Antebellum House Party

◇ ◇ ◇

To make the servant in the corner unobjectionable
Furniture, we must first make her a bundle of tree parts
Axed and worked to confidence. Oak-jawed, birch-backed,

Cedar-skinned, a pillowy bosom for the boss infants,
A fine patterned cushion the boss can fall upon.
Furniture does not pine for a future wherein the boss

Plantation house will be ransacked by cavalries or Calvary.
A kitchen table can, in the throes of a yellow-fever outbreak,
Become a cooling board holding the boss wife's body.

It can on ordinary days also be an ironing board holding
Boss garments in need of ironing. Tonight it is simply a place
For a white cup of coffee, a tin of white cream. Boss calls

For sugar and the furniture bears it sweetly. Let us fill the mouth
Of the boss with something stored in the pantry of a house
War, decency, nor bedeviled storms can wipe from the past.

Furniture's presence should be little more than a warm feeling
In the den. The dog staring into the fireplace imagines each log
Is a bone that would taste like a spiritual wafer on his tongue.

Let us imagine the servant ordered down on all fours
In the manner of an ottoman whereupon the boss volume
Of John James Audubon's *Birds of America* can be placed.

Antebellum residents who possessed the most encyclopedic
Bookcases, luxurious armoires, and beds with ornate cotton
Canopies often threw the most photogenic dinner parties.

Long after they have burned to ash, the hound dog sits there
Mourning the succulent bones he believes the logs used to be.
Imagination is often the boss of memory. Let us imagine

Music is radiating through the fields as if music were reward
For suffering. A few of the birds Audubon drew are now extinct.
The Carolina parakeet, passenger pigeon, and Labrador duck

No longer nuisance the boss property. With so much
Furniture about, there are far fewer woods. Is furniture's fate
As tragic as the fate of an axe, the part of a tree that helps

Bring down more upstanding trees? The best furniture
Can stand so quietly in a room that the room appears empty.
If it remains unbroken, it lives long enough to become antique.

from *The New Yorker*

My Husband

◇   ◇   ◇

My husband in the house.
             My husband on the lawn,
pushing the mower, 4th of July, the way
             my husband's sweat wends like Crown Royale
to the waistband
of his shorts,
             the slow motion shake of the head the water
running down his chest,
             all of this lit like a Poison video:
Cherry Pie his cutoffs his blond hair his air guitar crescendo.
My husband
at the PTA meeting.
             My husband warming milk
at 3 a.m. while I sleep.
My husband washing the white Corvette the bare chest and the soap,
             the objectification of my husband
by the pram pushers
and mailman.
             My husband at Home Depot asking
where the bolts are,
             the nuts, the screws,
my god, it's filthy
             my husband reading from the news,
             my husband cooking French toast, Belgian waffles,
my husband for all
nationalities.
             My husband with a scotch, my husband
with his shoes off,
             his slippers on, my husband's golden

leg hairs in the glow of a reading lamp.
My husband bearded, my husband shaved, the way my husband
                    taps out the razor, the small hairs
                                        in the sink,
                my husband with tweezers
to my foot,
        to the splinter I carried
for years,
                my husband chiding me
for waiting
to remove what pained me,
            my husband brandishing aloft
                    the sliver to the light, and laughing.

                from *Court Green*

A Common Cold

◊   ◊   ◊

A common cold, we say—
common, though it has encircled the globe
   seven times now handed traveler to traveler
   though it has seen the Wild Goose Pagoda in Xi'an
   seen Piero della Francesca's *Madonna del Parto* in Monterchi
   seen the emptied synagogues of Krasnogruda
   seen the since-burned souk of Aleppo

A common cold, we say—
common, though it is infinite and surely immortal
   common because it will almost never kill us
   and because it is shared among any who agree to or do not agree to
   and because it is unaristocratic
      reducing to redness both profiled and front-viewed noses
      reducing to coughing the once-articulate larynx
      reducing to unhappy sleepless turning the pillows of down,
         of wool, of straw, of foam, of kapok

A common cold, we say—
common because it is cloudy and changing and dulling
   because there are summer colds, winter colds, fall colds,
      colds of the spring
   because these are always called colds, however they differ
      beginning sore-throated
      beginning sniffling
      beginning a little tired or under the weather
      beginning with one single innocuous untitled sneeze
   because it is bane of usually eight days' duration
      and two or three boxes of tissues at most

The common cold, we say—
and wonder, when did it join us
   when did it saunter into the Darwinian corridors of the human
   do manatees catch them do parrots I do not think so
   and who named it first, first described it, Imhotep, Asclepius, Zhongjing
   and did they wonder, is it happy sharing our lives
      as generously as inexhaustibly as it shares its own
      virus dividing and changing while Piero's girl gazes still downward
      five centuries still waiting still pondering still undivided
      while in front of her someone hunts through her opening pockets for tissue
         for more than one reason at once

                    from *The Threepenny Review*

Crisis on Infinite Earths,
Issues 1–12

◇ ◇ ◇

.

'm at a poetry convention and wish I were at Comic Con. Everyone is wearing
oring T-shirts.

When I give the lady my name, she prints it wrong onto the name tag. I spell it and
he gets it wrong again. Let's be honest: it's still my fault.

I.

apanese tsunami debris
s starting to wash up
on the Pacific shore. At first,
hey trace back the soccer balls,

notorcycles, return them
o their owners. That won't last.
There are millions more tons.
Good news for beachcombers,

egins one news article.

III.

In the '30s, William Moulton Marston invented the polygraph and also Wonde
Woman. She had her own lie detector, a Lasso of Truth. She could squeeze th
truth right out of anyone.

Then things got confusing for superheroes. The Universe accordioned ou
into a Multiverse. Too many writers penned conflicting origin stories. Supe
strengths came and went. Sometimes Wonder Woman held the Lasso of Truth, an
sometimes she was just holding an ordinary rope.

IV.

Grandma was doing the dishes
when a cockatiel flew in the open window
and landed on her shoulder.
This was after the wildfire

took a bunch of houses.
Maybe the bird was a refugee,
but it shat everywhere
and nipped. She tried a while

to find to whom it belonged,
finally gave it away.
Then she found out
it was worth $800.

V.

Yeah, so there are a lot of birds
in poems these days.
So what? When I get nervous
I like to think of their bones,

so hollow not even pity or
regret is stashed inside,

eir bones like some kind
'invisible-making machine.

I.

that black Lab loping down the street the one someone called for all last night?

'iae-ton, *Ja*-cob, *An*-gel, or *Ra*-chel, depending on how near or far the man
opplered to my window.

II.

:an't decide which is more truthful, to say *I'm sorry* or *that's too bad*.

III.

ne family is living in a trailer
:xt to their burned-out house.
looks like they are having fun
thered around the campfire.

he chimney still stands
:e something that doesn't
now when to lie down.
ich driveway on the street

splays an address on a
rge cardboard swath, since
ere's nowhere else to post
e numbers. It's too soon

r me to be driving by like this.

IX.

Crisis on Infinite Earths (1985) cleared up 50 years of DC comic inconsistency, undi
the messy idea of the Multiverse. It took 12 issues to contain the disaster. The
surviving superheroes, like Wonder Woman, relaunched with a better idea of wh
they were. The dead stayed dead.

Now the Universe is divided neatly into pre- and post-Crisis.

X.

I confess stupid things I'm sorry for:

- saying that mean thing about that nice teacher
- farting in a swimming pool
- in graduate school telling everyone how delicious blueberry-flavored coffee from 7-11 was
- posing for photographs next to beached debris.

How didn't I know everyone liked shade-grown fair-trade organic?

XI.

I wish I could spin around so fast that when I stopped, I'd have a new name.

XII.

Here's a corner section
of a house washed up
on the shore, walls still
nailed together. Some bottles,

intact, are nesting inside.
I wasn't expecting this: ordinary
things. To be able to smell
someone else's cherry-flavored

cough syrup. There is
no rope strong enough
to put this back together.
To escape meltdown

at Fukushima-1, starfish
and algae have hitched rides.
They are invasive. What if
they are radioactive? Thank

goodness for the seagulls,
coming to peck out
everything's eyes.

from *New Ohio Review*

Body & Kentucky Bourbon

◊　◊　◊

In the dark, my mind's night, I go back
to your work-calloused hands, your body

and the memory of fields I no longer see.
Cheek wad of chew tobacco,

Skoal-tin ring in the back pocket
of threadbare jeans, knees

worn through entirely. How to name you:
farmhand, Kentucky boy, lover.

The one who taught me to bear
the back-throat burn of bourbon.

Straight, no chaser, a joke in our bed,
but I stopped laughing; all those empty bottles,

kitchen counters covered with beer cans
and broken glasses. To realize you drank

so you could face me the morning after,
the only way to choke down rage at the body

sleeping beside you. What did I know
of your father's backhand or the pine casket

he threatened to put you in? Only now,
miles and years away, do I wince at the jokes:

white trash, farmer's tan, good ole boy.
And now, alone, I see your face

at the bottom of my shot glass
before my own comes through.

from *Poetry Daily*

Exhibits from the Dark Museum

◇ ◇ ◇

In a shop of bloat and blown glass,
I pry an iridescent green beetle alive
from my ear and chase a dwindled trail

paved dire with coins towards three skulls
enclosed in a box of Olympia beer. Pale
grass: vitiligo thrust from the tract

of his scalp, now mine. Your voice,
a sforzando of light as it strikes the rock-
ridge hung above the dwellings.

Or, your voice, a grim notation of the sweep
between us. All night along with you
our sons respire. I fever through memory.

The world that survives me but a dangerous place.

from *Alaska Quarterly Review*

LAURA KASISCHKE

For the Young Woman
I Saw Hit by a Car While
Riding Her Bike

◇   ◇   ◇

I'll tell you up front: She was fine—although
she left in an ambulance because
I called 9-1-1

and what else can you do
when they've come for you
with their sirens and lights
and you're young and polite
except get into their ambulance
and pretend to smile?

"Thanks," she said to me
before they closed her up. (They

even tucked
her bike in there. Not
one bent spoke on either tire.) But I

was shaking and sobbing too hard to say good-bye.

I imagine her telling her friends later, "It

hardly grazed me, but
this lady who saw it went crazy . . ."

I did. I was
molecular, while
even the driver who hit her did
little more than roll his eyes, while

a trucker stuck at the intersection, wolfing
down a swan
sandwich behind the wheel, sighed. Some-

one touched me on the shoulder
and asked, "Are you all right?"

(Over
in ten seconds. She
stood, all
blonde, shook
her wings like a little cough.)

"Are you
okay?" someone else asked me. Uneasily. As if

overhearing my heartbeat
and embarrassed for me
that I was made
of such gushing meat
in the middle of the day
on a quiet street.

"They should have put *her*
in the ambulance, not me."

Laughter.
Shit happens.
To be young.
To shrug it off:

But, ah, sweet
thing, take
pity. One

day you too may be
an accumulation
of regrets, catastrophes.
A clay animation
of Psalm 73 (*But*

as for me, my feet . . .). No. It will be
Psalm 48: *They*

saw it,
and so they marveled; they
were troubled, and hasted away. Today

you don't remember the way
you called my name, so
desperately, a thousand times, tearing

your hair, and your clothes on the floor, and
the nurse who denied your morphine
so that you had to die that morning
under a single sheet
without me, in
agony, but

this time I was beside you.
I waited, and I saved you.
I was there.

from *Post Road*

In the End, They Were Born on TV

◊ ◊ ◊

i. good reality TV

a couple wanted to be -to-be and TV wants the couple-to-be
to be on TV. the people from TV believe we'd be good TV
because we had wanted to be -to-be and failed and now might.

to be good at TV make like TV isn't. make like living in our living room
and the TV crew isn't there and the boom isn't there
saving the woman from TV's voice that won't be there
saying *tell us about the miscarriage.* in the teeming evening
and some dog barking at all we cannot hear.

ii. would you be willing to be on TV?

people in their house on TV are ghosts haunting a house haunting houses.
pregnant women in their houses on TV are haunted houses haunting a house
        haunting houses.
our living room a set set for us ghosts to tell ghost stories on us.

would you be -to-be on TV?
to be the we we weren't to be and the we we're-to-be to be on TV.
the pregnant woman agrees to being a haunted house
haunting flickering houses. yes ok yeah yes.

iii. forms

in the waiting room for the doctor to TV the pregnant woman's insides
out on a little TV on TV. filling a form on TV is to flesh into words
on a sheet that fills up with you. yes yes and turn to the receptionist
only to turn back to a ghost waiting to be officially haunted yes.

a magazine riffles itself on TV; loud pages, a startled parrot
calls your name then alighting on magazines
and waddle the hall you -to-be and the TV crew that isn't going to be there
on TV and the doctor and you are looking at her little TV on TV the doctor
says *see? there they are.* ghosts sound themselves out to flicker on the little TV.
there they go to the pregnant woman scared to be such good TV.

iv. cut

to one-more-time-from-the-top yourself
is to ta-daaaaa breathing. the curtain drops, plush guillotine.
would you talk about the miscarriage one more time? ta-daaaaa

v. all the little people out there

after she was a haunted house before we haunted us for TV then
the pregnant woman watched TV. vomit on her teeth like sequins.

our TV stayed pregnant with the people from TV's TV show
pregnant with haunted houses wailing then smiling up into our living room.

it helps she said of the people from TV's TV show so *yes* then to TV to help,
she said, the haunted houses in the living rooms we said *yes* to help
thousands of wailing houses.

vi. only with some effort

the best ghosts trust they're not dead. no
no the best ghosts don't know how not to be alive.
like being good at TV.

inside the pregnant woman, the -to-be of the family-who-failed-
but-now-might-be-to-be were good TV.
but the we-who-failed butterfingered and stuttered,
held our hands like we just got them.

we've been trying so long we said *we can't believe it this is finally happening.*

vii. scheduled c-section: reality TV

and they're born made of meats on TV!
the doctor voilàs them from the woman's red guts
into the little punch bowls.

the new mother says *I want to see them my babies!*

the doctor shoves the new mother's guts back, express lane grocer.

the demure camera good TVs up two meat babies into wailing ghosts.

off, the new mother's blood like spilled nail polish.

viii. ghost story

did you know about dogs and ghosts? one barking at one's nothing?

ix. the miscarriage: exposition for reality TV

it helps to be on TV. we want to be good on TV. ok yes.
to help we want to be good TV. yeah yes.
please tell me about the miscarriage.

the woman from TV wants good TV and *something specific that gets you right
in the tear to the eye* to milk the pregnant woman's breasts heavy with—.

good, we talk about the dead one on TV.

it was horrible, the blood was everywhere that morning a dog barks.
one-more-time-from-the-top. *it was horrible, the blood was everywherrrr*
doggone dog goes on. on to take three and *it was horri*BOOM
in the boom goes the barking and bad TV! bad TV! we want to help
being good TV *please tell me about the miscarriage*
one more time *it was*

                    x. after the c-section was more like

the doctor shoving the new mother's guts in, jilted lover packing a
        duffel.

                xi. talking about the miscarriage: behind the scenes

please tell me about the miscarriage
please tell me about the miscarriage
please tell me about the miscarriage
please tell me about the miscarriage
the fifth take and *it was horrible*, that's all.
they call them takes, again we're robbed.

                            xii.

did it help watching a house fill with haunting every room
or help haunting the house? watch! here we are:
an expanding family of ghosts. we aren't here but yes ok yeah yes.
did it help? and even now know yes they were born on TV
but before *it was horrible* wasn't it must have been. please tell me
about the miscarriage for I don't know how not to be telling
and the dog growls still and still and still

                from *The Iowa Review*

Eating Walnuts

◇   ◇   ◇

The old man eating walnuts knows the trick:
You do it wrong for many years,
applying pressure to the seams
to split the shell along its hemispheres.

It seems so clear and easy. There's the line.
You follow the instructions, then
your snack ends up quite pulverized.
You sweep your lap and mutter, try again.

Eventually you learn to disbelieve
the testimony of your eyes.
You turn the thing and make a choice
about what you'd prefer to sacrifice.

You soon discover that the brains inside
are on right angles, so the shell
must be cracked open on its arc,
which isn't neat. The shattered pieces tell

a story, but the perfect, unmarred meat's
the truth: two lobes, conjoined, intact.
One of two things is bound to break:
One the fiction, one the soul, the fact.

from *Unsplendid*

DAVID KIRBY

Is Spot in Heaven?

◊ ◊ ◊

In St. Petersburg, Sasha points and says, "They're restorating
this zoo building because someone is giving the zoo an elephant
   and the building is not enough big, so they are restorating it,"

so I say, "Where's, um, the elephant?" and Sasha says,
"The elephant is waiting somewhere! How should I know!"
   When I was six, my dog was Spot, a brindled terrier

with the heart of a lion, though mortal, in the end, like all
of us, and when he died, I said to Father Crifasi, "Is Spot
   in heaven?" and he laughed and asked me if I were really

that stupid, insinuating that he, a holy father of the church,
had the inside track on heavenly entry, knew where
   the back stairs were, had mastered the secret handshake.

Later we saw a guy with a bear, and I said, "Look, a bear!"
and Sasha said, "Ah, the poor bear! Yes, you can have your
   picture with this one, if you like," but by then I didn't want to.

Who is in heaven? God, of course, Jesus and his mother,
and the more popular saints: Peter, Michael, the various
   Johns, Josephs, and Catherines. But what about the others?

If Barsanuphius, Fridewside, and Jutta of Kulmsee,
why not Spot or the elephant or the bear when it dies?
   Even a pig or a mouse has a sense of itself, said Leonard

Wolff, who applied this idea to politics, saying no single
creature is important on a global scale, though a politics
    that recognizes individual selves is the only one that offers

a hope for the future. Pets are silly, but the only world
worth living in is one that doesn't think so. As to the world
    beyond this one, as Sam Cooke says, I'm tired of living

but afraid to die because I don't know what's coming next.
I do know that Spot was always glad to see me, turning
    himself inside out with joy when I came home from school,

whereas Father Crifasi took no delight at the sight of me
or anyone, the little pleasure that sometimes hovered
    about his lips falling out of his face like the spark from

his cigarette when the door to the classroom opened
and we boys filed in as slowly as we could. Those
    years are covered as by a mist now, the heads of my parents

and friends breaking through like statues in a square
in a foreign city as the sun comes over my shoulder
    and the night creeps down cobblestoned streets toward

a future I can't see, though across the river, it's still dark,
but already you can hear the animals stirring:
    the first birds, then an elephant, a bear, a little dog.

from *The Cincinnati Review*

ANDREW KOZMA

Ode to the Common Housefly

◇ ◇ ◇

O Eternal Worrier, you strive to lick
your prints from every surface. O Six-Legged God,
O Tiny Resurrectionist, if I begged
you to stop, would you stop, would you nod

your clockwork head, would you promise to rot
in the corner after I've squashed you, silent
and uneager to raise your children from the dead.
Perhaps you aren't to blame, O Careless Parent.

You spread your seed only where it takes,
and I left the dishes uncleansed, the fruit
clogging the trash with its seductive scent.
Dogged Companion, you wear your dark suit

with pride, eager to mourn whatever dies.
I'm not your friend! You're not mine! What lies
we tell. I love the living, and you, the dead.
And here we are again, breaking bread.

from *Subtropics*

The Pickpocket Song

◇ ◇ ◇

Tickle a backside, friend, jiggle the wrist,
hither then sterling, then amethyst, onyx.
Eager spills eel-skin, python, seal-leather,
platinum and plate, all cabbage, all cheddar.
I say of the cutpurses: Straighten, and sing. Let us
carol each quick sticky digit, all ten,
                                    for my
kith can fleece your kin, and then some,
proudly and soundly, down sheer to the skin.

Only we dippers could psalm such a trilling,
cash-clips and coppers, all harmony belling.
Keen-fingered lifters, join in with them—
each bracelet, each necklace, each pearl-circled pin,
topaz and lapis, square perfect carats
swearing their ritzier whisper and pinch,
over and over the nimble thumb-catch.
Noble this music, good, noble, and able.
Grandeur for soul, chums, glad glory for table.

from *32 Poems*

DANA LEVIN

Watching the Sea Go

◊ ◊ ◊

Thirty seconds of yellow lichen.

Thirty seconds of coil and surge,
        fern and froth, thirty seconds
                of salt, rock, fog, spray.

                            Clouds
moving slowly to the left—

        A door in a rock through which you could see

                    —

another rock,
            laved by the weedy tide.

        Like filming breathing—thirty seconds

of tidal drag, fingering
            the smaller stones
                    down the black beach—what color

        was that, aquamarine?
Starfish spread

their salmon-colored hands.

                    —

I stood and I shot them.

I stood and I watched them
       right after I shot them: thirty seconds of smashed sea
           while the real sea

       thrashed and heaved—

       They were the most boring movies ever made.
I wanted
         to mount them together and press play.

—

       Thirty seconds of waves colliding.
Kelp

       with its open attitudes, seals
         riding the swells, curved in a row

       just under the water—

         the sea,
over and over.
         Before it's over.

from Poem-a-Day

See a Furious Waterfall Without Water

◇ ◇ ◇

Never has an empty hand been made
into more of a fist, and Waterfall Without
        it swings so hard it swings out
of existence. How will anyone get married
now, with no wall of water behind them?
How will Over Niagara Falls in a Barrel
marry Across Niagara Falls on a Tightrope?
Over the Falls would have worn a veil,
Across the Falls would have tied a tie,
hand in hand they would have poured
down the aisle to the sound of rustling
        silks. Later they would narrow
to a lovely neck, later they would make
a gentle elbow in the water, later
they would pour into a still round pool,
and dance for three minutes to what they
called music. Niagara Falls is a family
member. He is drunk for the first time
in a hundred years. "I don't call that music
I call that noise," would have screamed
Niagara Falls, right through his aquiline
family nose. All of Niagara's ex-lovers
are here. The World's Steepest Dive
stands up and says, "I've been diving
        so long now, and when will I hit?
When will you be there for me, Niagara?"

First Woman Behind the Falls stands up
so everyone can see her, so everyone
can see what has happened to her looks.
"You took the best day of my life,
                    Niagara." The World's
        Longest Breath-Hold stands up,
she loves him, she drew in her breath
the first time she saw him and never
breathed out again, not ever. The furious
waterfall without water he punches her
into tomorrow; the World's Longest
Breath-Hold is longer now and she calls
to him from the future, "You're here,
        you're roaring again where I am,
Tomorrow." Finally his first love the U-
Shape stands up. Stands up and she says,
"Niagara." The sound curves down and up
again, even the shape of her voice is a U.
"I don't call that music I call that noise,"
says the furious waterfall without water,
trembling at the very lip, unable to contain
himself, and there he goes roaring
                        back into her arms.

        from *A Public Space*

Party Games

◇   ◇   ◇

Might night right sight?
—Andrew Joron

The first thing she did after we blindfolded her
and turned her in circles by her shoulders

was lunge
for where she thought her target hung

and hit tree trunk instead, with one strike
against it split the stick

in half to jagged dagger
in her

fists. The donkey gently swayed
within reach, barely grazed

and staring straight ahead with the conviction
inherent to its kind at the horizon

that a gaze
implies,

paper mane fluttering in the breeze of a near miss,
belly ballasted with melting chocolate kisses,

drawn grin belying its
thingness, rictus

of ritual and craft. She's grinning
too, and laughing, regaining

her balance,
planting her feet in a samurai stance.

She brandishes her splinter.
There's no harm in letting her

take another turn
without turning

her around again.
We think we know how this ends,

how good it feels to play at this,
violence and darkness,

the beast
that harbors something sweet.

from *The Hopkins Review*

Anxieties

◇ ◇ ◇

It's like ants
and more ants.

West, east
their little axes

hack and tease.
Your sins. Your back taxes.

This is your Etna,
your senate

of dread, at the axis
of reason, your taxi

to hell. You see
your past tense—

and next? a nest
of jittery ties.

You're ill at ease,
at sea

almost in-
sane. You've eaten

your saints.
You pray to your sins.

Even sex
is no exit.

Ah, you exist.

from Poem-a-Day

If My Late Grandmother Were Gertrude Stein

◇   ◇   ◇

I. Southern Migration

Leech. Broke speech. Leaf ain't pruning pot. Lay. Lye. Lie. Hair straight
off. Arrowed branch and horse joint. Elbow ash. Row fish. Row dog.
Slow-milk pig. Blue-water sister. Hogs like willow. Weep crow. Weep
cow. Sow bug. Soul narrow. Inchway. Inches away. Over the bridge.
Back that way. Fur. Fir needles in coal. Black hole. Black out. Black
feet. Blame. Long way still. Not there. There. Here. Same.

II. Feed the Saw

Old Crow. Liquor. Drink. Drunk. Girdle. Grits. Grit. Tea. Grit tea.
Tea git. Get shaved. Shook. Shucked. Shit. Flour. Flower. Lard and
swallow. Hardedge chew. Chipped tooth bite. Tool chip. Bite. Bloat.
Bloat. Bloat. Blight seat. Blight sit tea. Be light city. Down town dim.
Slight dark. Old Arc. New Arc. New Ark. New work. Newark. Lark-
fed. Corned bread. Bedfeather back. Sunday-shack church fat. Greased
gloved. Dust-rubbed. Love cheap-heeled shoes. Window seat. Mirror
eye. Window. I. Window. Window. When though. When though. Wind
blow. November. December. No cinder. No slumber. No summer.
Branch. Branched. Blanched. Fried. Freed. Fly. Want. What. Want.
What. Graves want.

III. Miscegenation

Good. Smooth. Curly-haired baby. Baby rock-a-bye. My baby. Mama rock-a-bye that baby. Wrestle the earth, baby. No dirt. No. Dirt-shine. Shine. Shine-neck. Porcelain. Tin. Tarnish. Powder milk. Pout her. Milk. Powder-silk inheritance. Front the washtub. Top the bed. Bin. Leaky numbers run in. Run in. Run on. Red fevers hold your palm. Sweat it out. Hot. Hot. Heat the rest. Pretty melt that wax. Wide flower. Ellis-Island daddy. O, Daddy's bar. Banned. Mongrel hum. Come. Come now. Little bones bend. Old crack. Creak. Crank. Crick. Curly-Q. Fuck. Them. Then fuck them. You hear me. Walk through good-haired baby. Half of you. Belong.

IV. Gertrude Stein

Who. Bills mount. Picasso. Who. Matisse. Who. Mortgage. No currency canvass. Pay brushes. Stroke. Stroke. Bridge. Brittle. Blend. 10 miles daybreak. 10 miles they break. They broke. No brick. Widgets in the envelope. No railroad green. Agriculture. Pea snap. Earth under nails. Spine and stilt woman. Roach-kill heel woman. Roaches in the crawl. Woman, creep. Keep 5th grade. Every where. Wear every where. We're every. Where. Any. How. We sacrifice and hammer. They sacrifice the hammer. Never. Ax and hatchet make callous. Hard hand. Prison-pen privilege. Prison. Privilege pinned. Bar-thorn pinned. Pine cross. Crown. Weight. Wait. Iron is harder. Chicken fat can is full of spark. Spark kill. Ore. Sparkle. Or. Spark cull. Spark. Cull. Hoe. Heave. Heave-holy. Heavy. Heavy. Heavy lights genius. That is that Gertrude. Who.

from *Kinfolks Quarterly*

There Are Birds Here

◊　◊　◊

for Detroit

There are birds here,
so many birds here
is what I was trying to say
when they said those birds were metaphors
for what is trapped
between fences
and buildings. No.

The birds are here
to root around for bread
the girl's hands tear
and toss like confetti. No,

I don't mean the bread is torn like cotton,
I said confetti, and no
not the confetti
a tank can make out of a building.
I mean the confetti
a boy can't stop smiling about,
and no his smile isn't much
like a skeleton at all. And no
their neighborhood is not like a war zone.

I am trying to say
the neighborhood is as tattered
and feathered as anything else,
as shadow pierced by sun

and light parted
by shadow-dance as anything else,
but they won't stop saying

how lovely the ruins,
how ruined the lovely
children must be in your birdless city.

from *Poetry*

LAURA McCULLOUGH

There Were Only Dandelions

◇   ◇   ◇

And the boy.

Everywhere, sound. Here: sirens. There: sirens.
And the crying

> [because one woman's husband
> doesn't love her anymore
> and wants to go to medical school,
> now, after so many years of lawyering;
>
> because another one woke up one day,
> told her husband, *I don't think I ever want*
> *to sleep with you again*, meaning sex,
> and then he learned it meant not
> even the sleeping, the spooned, belly loose
> intimacy of howler monkey night;
>
> because the dandelion blew
> into a million parachuting seeds.]:

> Pre-dandelions floating everywhere, to every continent.
There, too, screaming, just like sirens,
> and everywhere in between, each anniversary of the living.

My boy is in college now, one says,
> *but that day of the bombing,*
> *when they called, I stopped at the 7–11*
> *to buy bags to bring the body parts home in.*
> *He was one of only four that survived.*

[Whose baby, anonymous, in the trash heap

Whose boys aiming, aiming, falling in love
with the fear they won't ever outrun?
Whose child that one,
without an arm, a knife in the other?]

They're not all white faces, and this poem
is not a public poem.
Not all poems are meant to entertain,
like Jericho said, named
after that city by that river
in the hot place so many people
have lived in, so many hostages
been taken in, so many,
so many—whose offices I can't name or know—
no, not entertain, but sing just the same,
a polyphony of song
birds in the morning,
snow geese aflight, guns rocketing,
barrel out, sound through
the beating blood,
bleating animals, beseeching
all those river gods
for some respite from this suffering.

[Each a lawn weed having grown
up in some crevice,
against the wall of each life,
flowering heads all in all
and each in one, this explosion
on the seed-headed planet,
fractal imagining, and this
is my imagining, this declaimed *I*]

Though some of you—
even though this is not a public poem—
will say the I is dead; there is no self;
no things but in ideas
dead, yet no ideas in things either;

and then the accumulation
of linguistic artifacts heats up like a
        like a like a
        lava lamp.
        [All Spencer's Gifts' glow and thrift store chic.]

And you will not be warmed by it,
        but who is this *you*?
        Because if there is no *I*,
        there can be no *we*,
and I am not willing to surrender to that.

        [to no *us-ness*, to you not being
        one sole being on the other end
        of this *this-ness*, but only part
        of some conglomerate, corporate
        entity called nothing-we-can-comprehend.
        I am unwilling;
        I am a dissenter.
        I am.]

Which renders the corporation something
        more than *they*,
        which is almost always paralytic or amoral,
        certainly unsympathetic and unsympathizable,
        something   approaching   evil.

Just you.   And me.   Please.

First, I claim this *I*, that only has this
        language(s), technology(s), space,
                time, sex, gender, religion
                    or lack thereof,
                    sensibility,   sense,
                        a body, a body in time,
                            in sex, in faith and betrayal
                                and reason and reasoning:

out of this great unsynthesized manifold,
        all penetration and penetrating.

[Like a seed head blown apart,
all pollination and flowering
and dried and falling away
and lifting and airborne and borne
away from each other to land
and germinate and survive
in the meagerness of conditions,
the little dying, the little survivals.]

An image, Williams said; an idea, said Stevens,
    ancestors we think of: lion's teeth leaves, prickly
    and persevering, no things but in ideas, really?

So much depends upon this small boy
    who doesn't look like any small boy you know;
he is my small boy—the I of this *this-ness*—
    with small bones and wide dark eyes,
    hair as straight and black as spun obsidian.

So much depends upon a child like him, this one I love,
    sitting in calf-high grass, so new-green, the edges
    blaze white, and the dandelions all sprung overnight,
    one night in this boy's newborn awareness,
    as new as any child's, burying his face in the common
    and undervalued florets, eyes blazing with YELLOW!!
    Mind cracking—everywhere this cracking—a portal
    into a new way of being, the dancing around him,
    the buzz of new insects, the spray of misting winds;

it is all so amazing, this world of wonder.

from *Verse Daily*

RAJIV MOHABIR

Dove

◇ ◇ ◇

chwa ke mare ordhniya ke torde,
har najariya jaherile jaherile

scorpion stings me; its toxins swim my veins,
ne ill prick from you and I writhe in your fever.

dream I cough up a songbird I release to the sky,
u board a plane to take you across the desert.

will tie messages to the feet of doves,
t them to sail at dusk with a map to your country.

izzy with thirst they fall, raining, from the sky,
eir dried meat hardening in tawny feathers.

throw stones at planes' shadows, cursing iron
crash, to burn in serrated-leafed cane fields.

my skin never blisters with your desire,
birdbaths I empty vials of avicide.

The scorpion's sting tears my veil,
the glance from your poisonous eyes.

from *Prairie Schooner*

99

Upon Hearing the News You Buried Our Dog

◇   ◇   ◇

I have faith in the single glossy capsule of a butterfly egg.
I have faith in the way a wasp nest is never quiet

and never wants to be. I have faith that the pile of forty
painted turtles balanced on top of each other will not fall

as the whole messy mass makes a scrabble-run
for the creek and away from a fox's muddy paws.

I have been thinking of you on these moonless nights—
nights so full of blue fur and needle-whiskers, I don't dare

linger outside for long. I wonder if scientists could classify
us a binary star—something like Albireo, four hundred

light-years away. I love that this star is actually two—
one blue, one gold, circling each other, never touching—

a single star soldered and edged in two colors if you spy it
on a clear night in July. And if this evening, wherever you are,

brings you face-to-face with a raccoon or possum—
be careful of the teeth and all that wet bite.

During the darkest part of the night, teeth grow longer
in their mouths. And if the oleander spins you still

another way—take a turn and follow it. It will help you avoid
the spun-light sky, what singularity we might've become.

from Poem-a-Day

Plutonium

◊　◊　◊

after Richard Rhodes

1

A man stood beside the gate
with his severed eyeball
in the palm of his hand.

The empty socket stared at me
with a shy creeping fire
or so I imagined in my pride.

So I said, "I can undo this."

2

*We watched the blast through welder's glass
and a tinted lens, from twenty miles east
in the Sierra Oscura. We slathered ourselves
with suntan lotion. Serber peeped
with a naked eye, and was blinded
for ninety seconds—when he could see again,
just chaparral and nine scrub pines.
The light had bounced off the moon.*

3

Neils Bohr recites in his soft rapt voice: *I divide myself into two persons, one of whom tries to fool the other, while a third, who is in fact the same as the other two, is filled with wonder at this confusion. Thinking becomes dramatic, and quietly acts the most complicated plots with itself and for itself; and the spectator again and again becomes an actor.*

4

The pile contains 771,002 pounds of graphite, 80,590 pounds of uranium oxide, 12,412 pounds of uranium metal, and took seventeen days to build. At 3:49 Fermi orders the control rods removed. At 3:53 he shuts the reaction down. It produced a half watt of energy, not enough to flicker a bulb, but the neutron intensity doubled every two minutes.

5

The guard stood aside, the eye in his hand
flinched, I lowered my head,
when I crossed that threshold
I was back in childhood, a swing rocked,
a red ball bounced, the little ones
were jumping rope and chanting
the numbers, holy names
that stand for nothing except themselves.

Thorium is sequenced from that song,
radium and the transuranic elements.

Once or twice they clapped.

Then it was night, my father called me home,
by no name or voice, just darkness.

from *The Manhattan Review*

54 Prince

◊　◊　◊

There exist 54 Goldilocks planets
54 planets not too hot
54 planets not too cold
54 planets where the living
is juuuuuust right
in that particular planetary zone

54 planets like Earth
but not Earth Similar
not the same 54 planets close
but different Different
except for Prince

Assless Pants Prince
High-Heel Boots Prince
Purple Rain Prince
Paisley Park Prince
I Would Die For You Prince
Ejaculating Guitar Prince
Jehovah's Witness Prince
Needs A New Hip Prince
Wrote *Slave* On His Face Prince
Took An Unpronounceable Symbol For His Name Prince
Chka Chka Chka Ahh Prince

54 planets each with a Prince
and every Prince
exactly the same
as the one we know on Earth

54 lace 54 canes
54 planets 54 Prince

These 54 Prince swallow 54 worries
The 54 worries become 54 songs
54 songs made of 54 bars 54 bars
using 54 chords 54 downbeats
where they pick up the worries
54 offbeats to lay the worries down again
54 worried skank-beat Prince
birth 54 worrisome funk-drenched songs

Once an Earth year the Prince
gather around Lake Minnetonka
When the cherry moon smiles
they thrust under their heads
Under the water the Prince sick up
the old worries Under the water
worry sacks rise empty again

It takes a worried man the Prince say
to sing a worried song
while beneath the surface of Lake Minnetonka
the perch in the shoals
and the gobies in their holes
nibble at the worries
our skimmed from the top worries
scraped from the bottom worries
spooned from the middle good enough worries
There's worries now the fish sing
but there won't be worries long

from *The Awl*

RON PADGETT

Survivor Guilt

◊　◊　◊

It's very easy to get.
Just keep living and you'll find yourself
getting more and more of it.
You can keep it or pass it on,
but it's a good idea to keep a small portion
for those nights when you're feeling so good
you forget you're human. Then drudge it up
and float down from the ceiling
that is covered with stars that glow in the dark
for the sole purpose of being beautiful for you,
and as you sink their beauty dims and goes out—
I mean it flies out the nearest door or window,
its whoosh raising the hair on your forearms.
If only your arms were green, you could have two small lawns!
But your arms are just there and you are kaput.
It's all your fault, anyway, and it always has been—
the kind word you thought of saying but didn't,
the appalling decline of human decency, global warming,
thermonuclear nightmares, your own small cowardice,
your stupid idea that you would live forever—
all *tua culpa*. John Philip Sousa
invented the sousaphone, which is also your fault.
Its notes resound like monstrous ricochets.

But when you wake up, your body
seems to fit fairly well, like a tailored suit,
and you don't look too bad in the mirror.
Hi there, feller!
Old feller, young feller, who cares?
Whoever it was who felt guilty last night,
to hell with him. That was then.

from Poem-a-Day

Candying Mint

◊   ◊   ◊

Strip thirty good-sized leaves.
Wash them, and pat dry.

Paint the leaves with egg white
and dredge in fine sugar.
Let stand upon a wire rack.

Buber writes, "man's final objective is this:
to become, himself, a law—a Torah."

The granules glimmer upon the mint,
hard dew, a glittery,
sweet finish to a fine night

and a flourless chocolate cake
with a little raspberry sauce.

I know that it's my job, but Rabbi, I worry
because I like worrying,
and I admire the persistence of the mint,

really just a weed: spicy, ragged, alive.
To grow toward the sun—it's like listening—

and who doesn't need to aspire?
Yes, Rabbi, the lesson's true:
to become a law means to know God,

but who could be ready for that?
Rabbi, try the candied mint: it's heaven.

from *The Carolina Quarterly*

Relevant Details

◇   ◇   ◇

The bar was called The Den of Iniquity,
or maybe The Cadillac Lounge—whatever
it was, its sign was a neon martini glass,
or a leg ending in stiletto. Maybe a parrot. Anyway,
in that place I danced without anyone
touching me but seven men watched
from the bar with embered, truculent eyes.
Or I danced with my boyfriend's hands
hot around my ribs. Or I didn't have a boyfriend
and no one was looking and my dance moves
were nervous, sick-eel-ish, and eventually
I just sat down. What I remember for sure
is that was the night I drank well gin
and spun myself into a terrible headache.
That was the night I thought I was pregnant
and drank only club soda. That was
the night I made a tower from Rolling Rock
bottles sometime after midnight
and management spoke to me quietly
but only after snapping a Polaroid
for the bathroom Wall of Fame. In any case,
when I finally stumbled or strode
or snuck outside, the air was Austin-thick,
Reno-dry, Montpellier-sharp. I don't remember
if my breath clouded or vanished
or dropped beneath the humidity. I don't remember
if the music pulsing from inside
was the Velvet Underground or Otis Redding
or the local band of mustached banjo men.

You know this poem has a gimmick,
and you're right. But understand: if I wrote
Cadillac Lounge, boyfriend, beer tower, soul
it would be suddenly true, a memory lit
by lightning flash. Who needs that sort
of confinement? If the way forward
is an unbending line, let the way back
be quicksilver, beading and re-swirling. Forgive
the trick and let me keep this mix-and-match,
this willful confusion of bars, of beaches,
of iced overpasses and hands on my hands,
all the films with gunfights, all the films
with dogs, the Kandinsky, the Rembrandt,
the moment the moon's face snapped
into focus, the moment I learned
the word *truculent*, each moment the next
and the one before, and in this blur,
oh, how many lifetimes I can have.

from *Pleiades*

The Main Event

◊　◊　◊

At the weigh-in
on the morning of March 24th, 1962, the World Welterweight Champ,
Benny "Kid" Paret,

called his challenger, Emile Griffith, a *maricón*—
Cuban slang for "faggot"—
and smiled. Emile wanted to knock the Kid out right there.

Gil Clancy, his manager,
managed to hold him back, told him to "save it for tonight."
The New York Times

wouldn't print the correct translation, maintained that Paret had called
Emile an "unman."
The sportswriter Howard Tuckner raved against the euphemistic

copy editors, "A butterfly
is an unman. A rock is an unman. These lunatics!"
No one would mention

the word "homosexual" in connection with a star
athlete. Another
journalist, Jimmy Breslin—Irish straight-talker—said,

"That was what Paret
was looking to do—get him steamed! If you're going to look for trouble,
you found it!"

By the twelfth round, both men had tired. They clinched, heads ear
                    to ear, embracing,
then punching underneath, whaling away at the other's

                    ribs, face. Such
intimate hostility. As if, could they have spoken to each other
                    through plastic mouth guards,

they would have groaned out curses, endearments, pillow talk.
                    At the close of the sixth round
the Kid had landed a combination, ending in a hard right

                    to Emile's chin.
He had gone down in his corner for an eight count,
                    but got back up

and started slugging as the bell rang and delivered him
                    from an almost certain
knockout. The crowd had shouted, whistled, roared.

                    In the black-and-white footage
of the TV broadcast on YouTube, the referee Ruby Goldstein breaks up
                    their clinch. Photographers

lean in and slide their old-fashioned flash-bulb cameras across the ring's
                    sweat-spattered
canvas floor to get a closer shot of the exhausted fighters. Cigarette

                    and cigar smoke
hangs heavy. The announcer Don Dunphy complains, "This is probably
                    the tamest round

of the entire fight." One second later Emile staggers the Kid
                    with an overhand right.
"Griffith rocks him." Emile lands twenty-nine punches in eighteen

                    seconds. "Paret against
the ropes, almost hopeless." Emile steps back, winds up, then swings
                    to get his full

body weight into each punch. Eyewitness Norman Mailer, ten feet
                    away from the fighters,
would write that Emile's right hand was "whipping like a piston rod

                    which had broken through
the crankcase, or like a baseball bat demolishing a pumpkin."
                    The crowd screams,

frenzied as piranhas stripping in less than half a minute the flesh
                    from a cow fallen
into the river. As Emile hammers the Kid's head with nine straight uppercuts

                    in two seconds, so it whips
back and forth in the slow-motion replay like a ragdoll's head shaken
                    by a girl throwing

a tantrum, one commentator observes, "That's beautiful
                    camera work,
isn't it?" Another responds, "Yeah, terrific." While Emile mauls

                    the Kid with mechanical
precision, he may be thinking of how the Kid reached out
                    and tauntingly patted

his left buttock, lisping *Maricón, maricón*, as Emile stood
                    stripped down
to his black trunks on the scales at the weigh-in. Or he may be thinking

                    of his job designing ladies'
hats in the Garment District. Attach that ostrich feather to the brim
                    of the blue boater, left hook,

pile-driver right. Lean into the punch. Put him away. But Paret,
                    tangled in the ropes,
won't go down. Clancy had told him to keep punching until

                    the referee separated
them. Emile doesn't know that the Kid will never regain
                    consciousness, will die

in ten days. He doesn't know that for the rest of his life
              he will have nightmares
in which he and Paret are marionettes. Someone jerks his strings. He can't

              stop punching. He will become
world champ four more times, but will himself be beaten almost
              to death by five young

homophobes, one with a baseball bat, as he leaves a gay bar near Port
              Authority. He will drive
a pink Lincoln Continental. After Paret's death, Manny

              Alfaro, the Kid's manager,
will say, "Now, I have to go find a new boy." His widow,
              Lucy, will bury him

in the St. Raymond Cemetery in the Bronx. She will never
              remarry, will tell an interviewer,
"Dream? I stopped dreaming a long time ago." Boxing matches

              will stop being televised
for the next decade. Ruby Goldstein will referee only one more fight,
              then retire. Emile

will suffer dementia pugilistica. He will be forced to sell his Continental
              and will ride the bus,
he'll say, "like everyone else." Benny Paret, Jr., the Kid's son

              who was two years old
when Emile killed his dad, will meet and forgive him forty-two years
              later. Lucy

had refused to go to the Garden or watch the fight on TV.
              A neighbor had to tell her.
Across nine million flickering screens nation-wide

              they hoisted the Kid's
still body onto a stretcher and carried him slowly out of the ring.
              Don Dunphy signed off,

"saying goodnight for your hosts, the Gillette Safety
              Razor Co., makers
of the $1.95 Adjustable Razor, super blue blades, foamy shaving

              cream, and Right Guard
Power Spray Deodorant, and El Producto, America's largest-selling
              quality cigar."

              from *Southwest Review*

CLAUDIA RANKINE

from Citizen

◇   ◇   ◇

Photograph courtesy of Michael David Murphy

Certain moments send adrenaline to the heart, dry out the tongue, and clog the lungs. Like thunder they drown you in sound, no, like lightning they strike you across the larynx. Cough. After it happened I was at a loss for words. Haven't you said this yourself? Haven't you said this to a close friend who early in your friendship, when distracted, would call you by the name of her black housekeeper? You assumed you two were the only black people in her life. Eventually she stopped doing this, though she never acknowledged her slippage. And you never called her on it (why not?) and yet, you don't forget. If this were a domestic tragedy, and it might well be, this would be your fatal flaw—your memory, vessel of your feelings. Do you feel hurt because it's the "all black people look the same" moment, or because you are being confused with another after being so close to this other?

An unsettled feeling keeps the body front and center. The wrong words enter your day like a bad egg in your mouth and puke runs down your blouse, a dampness drawing your stomach in toward your rib cage. When you look around only you remain. Your own disgust at what you smell, what you feel, doesn't bring you to your feet, not right away, because gathering energy has become its own task, needing its own argument. You are reminded of a conversation you had recently, comparing the merits of sentences constructed implicitly with "yes, and" rather than "yes, but." You and your friend decided that "yes, and" attested to a life with no turnoff, no alternative routes: you pull yourself to standing, soon enough the blouse is rinsed, it's another week, the blouse is beneath your sweater, against your skin, and you smell good.

The rain this morning pours from the gutters and everywhere else it is lost in the trees. You need your glasses to single out what you know is there because doubt is inexorable; you put on your glasses. The trees, their bark, their leaves, even the dead ones, are more vibrant wet. Yes, and it's raining. Each moment is like this—before it can be known, categorized as similar to another thing and dismissed, it has to be experienced, it has to be seen. What did he just say? Did she really just say that? Did I hear what I think I heard? Did that just come out of my mouth, his mouth, your mouth? The moment stinks. Still you want to stop looking at the trees. You want to walk out and stand among them. And as light as the rain seems, it still rains down on you.

from *Granta*

RAPHAEL RUBINSTEIN

Poem Begun on a Train

◊　◊　◊

Excuse me while I adjust the privacy settings of this poem
so that if it's ever published it will exist as a legible text
and not as a string of stubborn phrases I silently repeat to myself.
Three lines written, now three and a half, yet for the moment no one
but me has access to them, as they stretch haltingly
across the perfect grid of my Rhodia notebook,
unless, that is, Amtrak has installed
hidden video cameras above the seats in the coach class
of this Northeast Regional and one of them is focused on this very page.

Whoa, that idea came a little too easily.
The belief that your every move is being watched
used to be a sign of clinical paranoia,
except for those living under totalitarian regimes
in which case it was a perfectly reasonable assumption.
Now it's becoming a perfectly reasonable assumption
no matter where you breathe, no matter where you write.

Let's assume that Amtrak hasn't installed
individual video surveillance, at least not yet.
Let's further assume that this poem, which is slowly crawling from pure potential
to an intermediate state of being more concrete
than if I wrote it by fingertip on a steamy window
but less so than the station signs howling past,
has no other reader but me.
Still, once I transcribe my handwritten draft into my MacBook Pro,
a nearly inevitable step I am already contemplating
and will have long since accomplished by the time you read these lines

will have become so easily available to endless numbers
bureaucrats and hackers that I might as well post
e whole thing online immediately.

very poet thinks about every line being read by someone else
en if, as the line is written, its author suspects that he or she may die
fore those words will win the attention of any other human being.
siting a reader, sympathetic or dismissive,
apparently necessary for every poem,
om the most compressed, tongue-entangled lyric
stanzas as aerated and matter-of-fact as these.
here are times, however, when a reader is not merely posited
t becomes as factually undeniable as the poem itself.

hat's more, instead of turning a cold shoulder
bestowing ceremonial kisses on a prize-winner's cheeks,
is invisible reader rattles a set of prison keys
d is ready to dispatch an inconvenient text and author
a cold library with zero opening hours
om which nothing circulates except ashes.
o earn shelf space in this grim depository
oem doesn't even need to be written down.
hink of Mandelstam's "Stalin Epigram,"
lines recited to a few friends that signed their author's death warrant.
bviously, I don't have the slightest intention of comparing myself to Mandelstam
to any other poet writing within rifle shot of deadly auditors
or, for that matter, to Muhammad ibn al-Dheeb al-Ajami,
cently sentenced to life in prison (subsequently reduced to a mere 15 years)
r reciting a poem on YouTube that displeased the Emir of Qatar.

an't imagine any poem I might write coming with such a price,
t I live at a time when writing and its surveillance
ve become practically synonymous.
Discipline and Punish (original French title, *Surveiller et punir*)
oucault cites Bentham's panopticon prison
here an inmate can't know whether or not he or she
being watched by a guard at any given moment
must assume that observation is continual.
the present state of "carceral society" surveillance really is continual

and increasingly it is undertaken by the subjects themselves.
Fitbit, I read, is a small device to track your physical activity or sleep.
You can wear the device all day because it easily clips in your pocket,
pants, shirt, bra, or to your wrist when you are sleeping.
The data collected is automatically synched online when the device
is near the base station. After uploading, you can explore visualizations
of your physical activity and sleep quality on the web site.
You can also view your data using their new mobile web site.
You can also track what you eat, other exercises that you do, and your weight.

This is the world prophesied by Kenneth Goldsmith circa 1997
when he submitted himself to week-long audio surveillance
or attempted to describe his every physical action for a 13-hour period.
It's also the world embraced by a new generation of digital literary scholars
who employ data-mining techniques pioneered by the NSA.
True, poets have been engaged in "self tracking" for a long time.
"Let no thought pass incognito and keep your notebook
as strictly as the authorities keep their register of aliens," Walter Benjamin advise
They've also sometimes operated on the other side of the fence:
Wordsworth spying for England on his and Coleridge's 1798 trip to Hamburg,
Basil Bunting working undercover for British Military Intelligence
in Teheran until he was expelled in 1952.
But more often they have been the ones spied upon,
like Hugh MacDiarmid hounded in wartime Scotland
as a Communist agitator while he looked for "a poetry of facts."
At least he had the opportunity to lash back in a letter
to one of his tormentors, a certain Captain Jock Hay:
"It is intolerable that I should be subjected to inconvenience
and misrepresentation by a fatuous blowhard like you
and I have no intention of submitting to it,
even though the seriousness of it is mitigated by the fact
you are known as a windy ass and egregious buffoon
and not taken seriously by anyone who knows you."
(Andrew McNeillie, "A Scottish Siberia," *TLS*, Sept. 13, 2013.)

In *The Prelude*, Wordsworth was baffled at "how men lived
Even next-door neighbours, as we say, yet still
Strangers, not knowing each other's name."
Now I know the names of a thousand "friends" I've never met, and they mine,

o what do I have to hide from any device capturing these lines
o a distant database? My mind is filled with eavesdroppers and spies.
think a thousand times, or not a second, before I commit to a phrase
nd leave trails of metadata I'm asked to believe no one will ever pursue.
Rather than wallow in outmoded subjectivities
aw and naked to those unseen all-seeing eyes
naybe it's better to simply claim existing chunks of language
s MacDiarmid did in the Shetland Islands in the early 1940s
ranscribing lengthy passages from the *TLS*
or his eventually abandoned megapoem
"Cornish Heroic Song for Valda Trevlyn."
n June 1940 the authorities judged him "a case for continued observation"
nd in the following March put him on the "invasion list."
"It is probably unnecessary," Brooman-White wrote to Major Peter Perfect
Box 5, Edinburgh) on March 16, 1941, "as no doubt the local Police and Military
re all standing round waiting to pounce on him,
out to make assurance doubly sure, it might be as well to have his name added.
think we have plenty of evidence to justify this
out if you like I will send you up a summary of our file against the man."

The character Iris Henderson (Margaret Lockwood) in Hitchcock's *The Lady*
        Vanishes,
eleased in 1938, the year Mandelstam died,
s having tea in the dining car with the charming
out penniless musicologist Gilbert Redman (Michael Redgrave)
when she glimpses the name that Miss Froy (Dame May Whitty)
aad left on the window, a second before it vanishes.
She bolts from the table and desperately addresses the travelers around her:
"I appeal to you, all of you—stop the train. Please help me.
Please make them stop the train. Do you hear?
Why don't you do something before it's too late?"
Redgrave and duplicitous psychiatrist Dr. Harz (Paul Lukas)
attempt to restrain her but she breaks away.
Before pulling the train's emergency cord and collapsing in a dead faint,
he cries out: "I know! You think I'm crazy, but I'm not.
For heaven's sake, stop this train. Leave me alone. Leave me alone."
Amid the fascist shadows she is driven to hysteria
because a text has vanished before it could acquire other readers.

At the Whitney's "Rituals of Rented Island"
I walk into the Squat Theatre installation, suddenly remembering
evenings of radical performance circa 1979
as a long-forgotten line from one of Kafka's parables
hisses around me in low-fi analog:
"Nobody could fight his way through here even with a message from a dead man.

from *Harper's*

Endnotes on Ciudad Juárez

◇ ◇ ◇

1. The larger portion of this text discusses El Paso, Texas, the boring sister to Ciudad Juárez, México.
2. There are apartments that feel like they are by the sea, but out the window there is only freeway.
3. The geraniums always wilt either from heat or pollution.
4. El Canelo is the red-headed Mexican boxer who speaks Spanish.
5. Sometimes the candles are religious, sometimes they are not.
6. The girl from Juárez is beautiful. The girl from Juárez is God.
7. The tortilla border has shanties on one side and trailers on the other.
8. Some call them Fronchis because their license plates read: Fron-Chi for Frontera Chihuahua. Some just call them fresas.
9. In summer, roaches cross the street and travel home to home like people.
10. Campestre, Anapra, Chaveña, Anahuac, Flores Magon, and Independencia are only some of the neighborhoods in Ciudad Juárez.
11. Some streets are lined in wires because it's so easy to steal electricity.
12. Moxas graffiti walls: mee aamooo!! noo aa laas coopiioonaas!!
13. Some days saliva evaporates from the tongue.
14. The river has become the only blue vein left pulsing on the map.
15. The river is only blue on the map.

from *West Branch*

legend

◊   ◊   ◊

fern wept, let her eyes
    wet her tresses, her cheeks,
        her feet. the cheerlessness

    rendered her blessed,
strengthened her nerve.
    even then, she'd seen

        she needed her regrets
    melted. the weep-fest
helped her shed her tender

    edges, she felt the steel
        emerge. she'd served her
    sentence. she'd get herself

west, persevere, exert
    herself. they'd tell bess—
        her sweet bess!—fern'd

    deserted her. bess knew
better! when she left, fern
    pretended phlegm, yet

        she'd pledged she'd never
    rest ere she freed bess:
the excellent secret they

kept between themselves.
　　　　　when fern'd netted the
　　needed green, she'd send

bess her debt fee—then,
　　　　pressed, they'd sell her . . .
　　　　　　her self. (senseless!) *see*,

　　　　bess, she'd greet her when
they re-met, necks nestled,
　　　　flesh welded, essence-deep,

　　　　　　we knew we'd effect the deed!
　　　we're the bee's knees! they'll
never see cleverer femmes.

　　　from *Fence*

CHARLES SIMIC

So Early in the Morning

◊   ◊   ◊

It pains me to see an old woman fret over
A few small coins outside a grocery store—
How swiftly I forget her as my own grief
Finds me again—a friend at death's door
And the memory of the night we spent together.

I had so much love in my heart afterward,
I could have run into the street naked,
Confident anyone I met would understand
My madness and my need to tell them
About life being both cruel and beautiful,

But I did not—despite the overwhelming evidence:
A crow bent over a dead squirrel in the road,
The lilac bushes flowering in some yard,
And the sight of a dog free from his chain
Searching through a neighbor's trash can.

from *The Paris Review*

SANDRA SIMONDS

Similitude at Versailles

◊　◊　◊

Welcome to Humanities 203!
Here you will find the mysterious
      death of the honeybee, the Byzantine emperor,
Justinian, who made church and state
a seamless whole. Quiz tomorrow.
When someone dies, you buy their relatives flowers.
1-800-FLOWERS. As a result
your driving privilege will be suspended
      indefinitely on 11/13/2012.
            Where's mommy?
I said I was trying to write this poem
for the day, do you mind?
The Real Ghostbusters will return
      after these messages. The trap's ready.
I can get a girlfriend anytime I want.

On the toddler bed, wrapped in the felt
      blanket with monkeys printed all over it,
            their prehensile tails curled—
      I promise guys, I'll never let myself
get carried away by women again. I want pancakes.
Hey Sandra, I think Charlotte might be hungry.
      I'll be there in a second.
      Okay, I'll just feed her now.

      —what could pass as love inside capital?
Maybe just these records, the real.
      At the Halloween festival, my friend dressed
      her child as one of the 1%. Ezekiel

129

was a pirate. Her little girl threw
                fake bills into the air. She danced
in her suit and mustache. Thought—
    it will only ever snow $ in Florida

and you seemed more like the bas-relief,
the minor key, some detail about Louis XIV's
    weak blood I always forget to teach,
    and for a moment I had become
the anarchy of the sea—you know how the waves
are always pounding out some polyphony
        in saltwater, algae and fish
        that their subjects cannot understand.

from *Colorado Review*

ED SKOOG

The Macarena

◊ ◊ ◊

The chair I'm sitting on is mostly nothing.
Electrons go right through it. Memory, which
is electricity, seems like less than anything
and yet in the inexplicable universe I'm there
again, and it's now, the summer of the Macarena.
Two months in Abilene, Kansas, and I see
nobody in the central air of the Sunflower Hotel.
My eighth-floor window stares at soft, buttery hills.
Streetlights pink the tracks downtown
like a chalk outline to fill in later.
I never know what next. I am writing a novel.
Its characters are historians at the Eisenhower Library.
I go to its chapel daily, sit before his tomb
looking for a way to make a story up. I write
hundreds of pages, there and at my kitchenette,
alone and twenty-three. Some weekends I drive
to KC, where a woman who won't need me
lets me stay over, though at sex I'm still a boy,
the way at writing I'm still naïve, unskilled,
fascinated by form but lazy about content.
I'd like to finally read what I've been quoting.
Rummaging after maturity, I overdo the easy
and am too timid to engage full heart.
But I work the paths that may lead from myself.
Ike stays a boy, boyishly winning the worst war.
As president little happened we praise him for,
and by *we* I mean the characters of my novel,
among the adult troubles they fall into
and I don't understand. I avoid addressing

tyranny and battlefield and Holocaust.
For years I write liner notes to real life.
All drafts of that story will leave the earth,
and I'll send gratitude to the devil of fortune,
who will let that manuscript drift
like a bad vapor through offices of agent and editor.
This summer at the Democratic Party Convention
in Chicago, where the man who gives *Leaves of Grass*
away carelessly will be renominated, the delegates
keep doing the Macarena every time I look.
The vice president claims during his speech
to be doing the Macarena, but does not move,
then offers to demonstrate it again. Presidents
are always late in the day of their time.
Like dances, our political lives come and go.
It's the summer of all dances, coffee leaping
in the percolator, gravity-defiant solitude,
and through the window, houses and fields
seduced in their own passing crazes
of seasons, life and death that won't need me.

from *Fruita Pulp*

Ajar

◇   ◇   ◇

The washing machine door broke.   We hand-washed for a week.
Left in the tub to soak,   the angers began to reek,
And sometimes when we spoke,   you said we shouldn't speak.

Pandora was a bride;   the gods gave her a jar
But said don't look inside.   You know how stories are—
The can of worms denied?   It's never been so far.

Whatever the gods forbid,   it's sure someone will do.
And so Pandora did,   and made the worst come true.
She peeked under the lid,   and out all trouble flew:

Sickness, war, and pain,   nerves frayed like fretted rope,
Every mortal bane   with which Mankind must cope.
The only thing to remain,   lodged in the mouth, was Hope.

Or so the tale asserts—   and who am I to deny it?
Yes, out like black-winged birds   the woes flew and ran riot,
But I say that the woes were words,   and the only thing left was quiet.

from *The Atlantic Monthly*

Memo to the Former Child Prodigy

◊　◊　◊

by the age of nine　　you knew everything　　tra-la
had met two Presidents　　tra-la　　could explain pi

memorize Shakespeare soliloquies
or checkmate anyone blind-folded　　child's play

violin　　oboe　　harpsichord　　duplicate bridge
so what　　then　　was left to do

cut corners　　fit in　　marry someone
polish silver　　slap your children　　or go back

back to one　　tra-la　　then two and so forth
'til you learn to love all that blooms in the spring

from *Denver Quarterly*

Delicatessen

◊　◊　◊

after Hurricane Sandy & 3 nights of no power

In the delicatessen a last avocado.
Black, pulpy—a kind of soft grenade.

I set it down
for probably nobody.

I step out—not through doors
but through clear plastic tatters
shimmering in a doorframe.

Hothouse roses on the shelves outside;
hyacinths in foiled cups.

★

Calling storms by dumb names—
not the shabbiest way of neutering disaster,
I think.
　　　Like the pit bull called Cuddles,
the Lover's Lane near the sewage treatment plant—

Even *All Saints' Day*,
when you think about it.
Today, when I say, *I have it good*,
meaning, *better than others*,

& the children screaming *Help*
then *Made you look*, meaning
We tricked you—

★

But hyacinths in November!
You should see them!

Hyacinths make roses ridiculous by contrast.

Just look at the roses
hyperventilating in their cellophane shawls—

Pluck their cat claws & they don't object . . .

I want to grab someone passing & ask
the riddle that flowers won't answer—
how much beauty
comes from never saying no?

★

Maybe someone *will* answer me.
That's why I keep my mouth shut.

★

But not the sour-mouthed cashier—
she handles the bills,
she carelessly dabs the lemon wedge
she keeps by the side of the register.

Never a word from her.
Maybe the balances chafe
the tongue as well as the fingers.

She doesn't need to keep an eye peeled—
the cameras do it all.

If I could teach one art, it
would be how to go home unanswered,
empty-handed—

★

But what about the sidewalk Cyclops,

the all-seeing tattoo on the bald guy's head,
who once, I swear, called me by my right name,

who saw me frowning in sunlight—

*That & this so bad, Tyrell, you ain't
seen the darkest yet . . .*

The subway's closed tonight—
what darkest dark can he guard now?

★

I think I'd grow to like it—

the terrible wisdom
of stillness. The stomach, unchurning,
hollow as a prop.

The circles moving around them,
the cashier & the Cyclops.
The flowers too, if they can
reckon up anything besides their own mutilation.

Maybe they can sense
the babies wheeling by at warp speed . . .

who seem too light, having
little to them, or too much—an eye,
a name, some inarticulate rage,
all that's needed to be called a storm.

★

And what's a blackout, Tyrell?
Afraid of roaches?
Maybe you'll make some new friends.

★

And why hyacinths, why November?
Why rooted, not cut through, uncovered,
combining two colors?

Celestial blue, arterial purple,
maybe earth thinking both of heaven
& the blood in the sexes—

Thinking not only of a man-boy
turned into something beautifully inhuman
because a god looked at him once

but also picturing women
who know how to hide,

the woman in the jungle camp called
Hyacinth?

76, secreting herself
under a cot while the cult leader
in the pavilion makes nine hundred others
lie on the ground one last time,

& they won't rise again,
the cups on the ground like white flowers.

The toxins, red and purple in the cups,
around the roses of their mouths.

& Hyacinth who knows how to hide,
how to wait for the last to drink
even as the writer of the last note

summons those particulars
that are terrible for being so ordinary—

a gray sky, a dog barking,
a bird on a telephone wire.

White night, the leader calls it.

Stepping over the people on the ground—
Hyacinth & the moon
can rise in the white, humid night.

★

November then;
November now.

A kind of soft grenade
I set down for probably nobody.

Would I eat the goddamn flowers
if I thought they'd answer?

Made you look is all we can say

from *The Iowa Review*

How You Might Approach a Foal:

◊　◊　◊

like a lagoon,
like a canoe,
like you

are part earth
and part moon,
like déjà-vu,

like you
had never been
to the outer brink

or the inner Louvre,
like hay,
like air,

like your mother
just this morning
had combed a dream

into your hair,
like you
had never heard

a sermon or
a harsh word,
like a fool,

like a pearl,
like you
are new to the world.

from *The New Criterion*

S I D N E Y   W A D E

The Chickasaw Trees

◊   ◊   ◊

are full of bees
the pretty white

panicles
everywhere

light
turn them

frantic
as they haul

their pollen
baskets

from star
to star

to fragrant
star this

industry
thrumming

in the hearts
of flatland

plums hums
in the lucky

air far
from where

war
goes on

and on and
here on

the sun-lit
prairie light

winds shift
and dusky

nouns are sung
from the trees

where an owl
frowns

in sleep
and later

comes
in the guise

of ghost
to say

he knows
that all

the people
in a world

without bees
are lost

from *Blackbird*

Trades I Would Make

◇   ◇   ◇

Ronald Reagan for Donald Fagen.
Tijuana for Madonna.
This vale of tears for ten good years.
This schmuck I picked up in Indonesia for a bucket of anesthesia.
An icicle for a bicycle.
My neighbor's hollyhock trellis for Dock Ellis.
Jim (or Jimmy-o, if he'll permit) DeMint for a bit of lint.
A pay-as-you-go princess (read: overpriced hotté) for an iced latte.
A booster seat for some rooster meat.
A year in jail for some kale.
A turtle (either box or leatherhead) for a feather bed.
Gehrig, Unitas, Chamberlain (a bunch of dead jocks) for lunch with Redd Foxx.
A cat named Frisky for a vat of whiskey.
The color red for a feller named Jed.
A crate of elastic for a second-rate spastic.
A "C'mon, Cody, that's not very PC" shellacking for (and why not?) the Academy
     of American Poets' backing.
The Jackie Gleason Diet for a little peace and quiet.
Someone who dislikes (unlike us) *V* for a ficus tree.
An acceptable level of risk for a bowl of lobster bisque.
Former Seattle Seahawk and current KIRO newscaster Steve Raible for a tucked-
     away-in-the-corner-and-absolutely-not-double-booked New Year's Eve
     table.
Target (the store) for a degree in folklore.
The Business Section of *The New York Times* for a few more rhymes.
My imprisoned twin (and please, treat him nice) for Jim Rice.
A toy train (toot, toot) for a zoot suit.
A surfer-turned-robber's botched bank job ("gnarly") for Bob Marley.

hese "Good God, I'm suddenly feeling cold and sick" shivers for "Mick the Quick" Rivers.

he voices in my head for Joyce's "The Dead."

damaged and circling Space Shuttle that NASA won't let dock for a pet rock.

My EVIL THOUGHTS (evil; did I stammer?) for a hammer.

ticket to Loserdom for some booze or gum.

ticket to Nowhere for a stern warning: Don't Go There.

lectronica rap for a quick, uh, nap.

punch in the ear for a buncha beer.

My girlfriend's personality-test result ("Freako Chick," which quite shocked her) for Ferdie Pacheco, the quick-stitch Fight Doctor.

rotten grin for a cotton gin.

n irresponsible payout for a possible way out.

hanging slider for a spider.

resident William "Who Wants to Fight?" Howard Taft for a Million-Points-of-Light–powered raft.

ny two items of choice apparel (coats, stockings, pants) for Joyce Carol Oates's mocking glance.

One of those hard-to-believe jobs (gaffer? third mate?) for a buffalo-herd gate.

oday's sorrows for tomorrow's.

Overheard speech by Shakespeare when he was drunk and distracted (minor quotes) for you-can't-really-say-that-about-Zeppelin redacted liner notes.

ome bullshit homeroom teacher no one wants for a home-run hitter who also bunts.

Hey, choose me" pandering for some woozy meandering.

Jolly round the house for a Muhammad Ali roundhouse.

This nearly spent pen for some I-have-no-idea-where-the-time-went Zen.

he porn version of *The Little Engine That Could* for the possibility of making good.

A "Death, where is thy sting?" tattoo for, I don't know, something taboo.

A table at any of the nearby Benihanas for ten iguanas.

A too-sweet dessert—say, a snickerdoodle—for a too-precious craft-piece—say, a wicker poodle.

A Roman brick ruin for a romantic shoo-in.

omeone mistaking me for Lance Armstrong ("Hi, Lance!") for silence.

A Fujitsu waterproof shower phone (or a dour crone) for an hour alone.

ome honest-to-God (God? You bet) belief for some debt relief.

The freakish good luck of Arthur Conan Doyle for, fuck, anyone loyal.

Fred Astaire for bus fare.

My two-timin' great-uncle for Simon & Garfunkel.

A bought-in-the-Market-Square mini-drum for the bare minimum.

My favorite Yeti for Dave Righetti.

A thoughtless—uh-oh!—clown for a throwdown.

Any kind of already-banned quota for Manny Mota.

My iPhone, my Swiffer, my fogless mirror, anything that is, I swear to you,
  shoddy, for a "Whatever, it was hot when I brought it to you" toddy.

John Travolta, Gabe Kaplan, or Lawrence Hilton-Jacobs (really, any *Welcome
  Back, Kotter* entertainer) for a Bangladeshi otter trainer.

An almond steamer for a lemur.

Some long-suppressed gossip about former Baltimore Mayor Kurt (which is how
  he still likes to be addressed) Schmoke for your best joke.

A major-sized mystery caper for a plagiarized History paper.

The ghost of Truman for some roasted cumin.

Anything from a church (the altar, a splash of Holy Water, the wood pews) for
  some good news.

Anything reckoned dear for a second beer.

The dropping of charges (reckless endangerment, indecent exposure) for closure.

A "Dear Twit" letter for something a bit better.

The less-than-distinguished GOP field for a DiCaprio biopic: *Leo, Revealed*.

The blessèd (I do reckon) dead for your second-best bed.

A drawer of dimes for some more rhymes.

A veiled promise of matrimony from Mr. Met ("I do, but not yet") for a true tête-
  à-tête.

The righteous man's path (Thank Christ!) for the aftermath of a bank heist.

Bounty, the quicker picker-upper, for some no-count count's Brie-with-liquor-
  kicker supper.

A cup of roux for a schtup or two.

A battle-tested cry ("Let us in!") for the rest of my medicine.

A brand-new wok for Lou Brock.

An ain't-I-wild, flapper-style milieu for a childnapper who aims to steal you.

A complicated fate (healthy, books well reviewed, but penniless, and stuck on a
  street corner, forced to beg, alone) for a megaphone.

A game of catch for an aimless letch.

The bark of a seal for anything real.

Faye Dunaway for a foreign—"How you say?"—runaway.

A staggering ("Just one last swig") Billy Joel for a big chili bowl.

A "Baby baby what's the matter?" kiss for that or this.

My ex-girlfriend (a pill-popper, a lout, a jaw-clencher) for a kill-or-be-killed
    proper outlaw adventure.
These constant cries of "Why, God?" for a colossal-sized tripod.
Anyone from the rougher parts of Paris for anyone dumb enough to spare us.
Some this-is-so-good-you-must've-made-it-in-culinary-school chocolate for a
    multi-tool player who'll walk a lot.
A tipsy poodle for some dipsy-doodle.
Any ridiculous status (executive! platinum! wined and dined! preferred!) for a
    kind word.
The straight and narrow for a great sombrero.

from *Poetry Northwest*

Goodness in Mississippi

◊   ◊   ◊

after Gwendolyn Brooks's "We Real Cool,"
with thanks to Terrance Hayes

My friend said I wasn't fat but she was, and we
would go on that way, back and forth. She was my first real

friend, the kind who changes everything. Her mother was so cool,
didn't shave down there for the country club pool where we

sat beside her. I saw a gleam of her secret, silver hair and was left
dreaming of lime floating in a clear drink. I started saying hi at school

and people smiled back. Smile first, my friend said, and we
were a team. The cheerleaders who would always lurk

by the field, showing off their muscled legs—of late
I'd hardly noticed them. We talked about art, we

attended science camp in Gulfport. That's where her mother got struck
by a car the next year. She must have thrown the new baby straight

as a football to save her. Their family was on vacation, and we
found out at Sunday School, waiting for the choir to sing.

She was so good she comforted *me*. People saying, "It's just a sin,"
her mom like Snow White under glass, red lipstick, platinum hair we

knew was genetic. You'll still look young, I said. I think you're thin.
We'd skip lunch, drink Sego ("good for your ego"). Last year I drank gin

and called her ex. "She passed," he drawled, like it was the weather. We
tried powdered donuts with the Sego, sweated to the Beatles and jazz.

Her whole life was beginning. We moved away from there one June,
Mississippi tight-mouthed as a lid on fig preserves. And we—

we white girls—knew nothing. The fire-bombed store, the owner who died
for paying his friends' poll taxes. Anorexia would be famous soon.

from *The Georgia Review*

City of Eternal Spring

◊　◊　◊

My mind rises up as the silos of interchanges,
streams, passages of myself in floating layers
so nothing can connect, and I dream emptiness
on ships sailing to new places for new names,
this ship my hands cupped in front of me,
a beggar's bowl, a scooped out moon, a mouth
opened to make noiseless screams, to arrange,
to begin, to break through to stop my arrogance,
believing what I touch, see, feel, hear, taste make
a case for being alive, so I can stop believing what
happens when a caterpillar dreams itself beautiful.

What cannot be is suddenly what I was made
to believe can never be, fibers growing in illegal
spaces between layers of who I am and I wake
from nightmares that come at night or in the day,
memories of being betrayed gathering like iron
threads to make a prison where fibers of a miracle
of light crack open in a seed inside love to let me
dream a body inside this body with structures
that breathe and know one another so I rise
from thought to be being beyond thought
with energy as breath, a world with eyes
opening inside the light, inside knowing,
inside oneness that appears when the prison
frees me to know I am not it and it is not me.

from *The Rumpus*

CANDACE G. WILEY

Dear Black Barbie

◊　◊　◊

I made you fuck my white Barbie
even though I knew you didn't want to.
There were no whips or chains,
this was a different kind of plantation fantasy.
I didn't have a Ken doll, so I made you the man.
Not knowing what fucking looked like
I just rubbed you against each other and made you kiss.

I kept you barefoot like you came
three worlds later or fifty years earlier,
but I had Nicki Minaj dreams for us:
bleached brown skin, long stringy yellow hair,
God-blue eyes, lips pink as a Cadillac. Only then
could you wear the best dress and the one pair of pumps.

My dear black Barbie, maybe you needed a grandma
to tell you things are better than they used to be.
There was a time when you didn't exist at all.

from *Prairie Schooner*

TERENCE WINCH

Subject to Change

◇ ◇ ◇

Let us shove the last 73 minutes down the garbage
disposal and vacuum up all traces of the past 17 years
and stuff them in a plastic bag and be done with them.
Let's scrape our alternative versions of everything
we have learned since 1981 off the ground and flush
them all down the toilet. I'm worn out by my misdeeds.
My hands hurt, my fingers won't curl anymore.
I'm in the emergency room at Holy Cross hoping
all is not lost. I have no one to pray to, just the vast
empty sky, the black hole inside the black hole
that swallows up everything whole. They make
me lie down on the blank slate. Dr. Baker is running
late. Then the nurse lifts the curse and Baker says
you're a lucky man. It could have been worse.

from *Beltway Poetry Quarterly*

Thaw

◇   ◇   ◇

The trees glowed in water

I had half an ice arm

I waved at the sun for warmth and connection

This melting chandelier of mine

A fever grew from my ankles up

A planet fell out of my mouth

My organs bloomed, parachutes in the night

Snowbells rang along my teeth

My verbs were all in disagreement

Swallowed up in the turbulence

In the rotten rumble of boiling eggs

I held the cold along the eyelashes of cows

I held my rosehip head, splitting in two

To remain perpetually aware

A feather suspended itself in air

The fish sitting too long in the sun melted

Into a sea, cell after cell

My prized imperatives, my root words: gone

Long live the day

from *Birdfeast*

March of the Hanged Men

◊   ◊   ◊

1.

hyperarticulated giant black ants endlessly boiling out of a heaped-up hole
    in the sand

2.

such a flow of any other thing would mean abundance but these ants replay
    a tape-loop vision

3.

out of hell the reflexive the implacable the unreasoning rage whose only end
    is in destruction

4.

the way the dead-eyed Christ in Piero's *Resurrection* will march right over
    the sleeping soldiers

5.

without pausing or lowering his gaze for he has no regard now for human
    weakness

6.

since that part of him boiled entirely away leaving only those jointed
    automatic limbs

7.

that will march forward until those bare immortal feet have pounded a path
    through the earth

8.

back down to hell because there is no stopping point for what is infinite what
    cannot be destroyed

from *The Paris Review*

CONTRIBUTORS' NOTES AND COMMENTS

SARAH ARVIO was born in 1954. She grew up not far north of New York City and lived in the Village for thirty years. She has published three books of poetry, *Visits from the Seventh*; *Sono: cantos*; and *night thoughts: 70 dream poems & notes from an analysis*, which is a hybrid of poetry, essay, and memoir (all from Alfred A. Knopf). She has won the Rome Prize of the Academy of Arts & Letters and fellowships from the Bogliasco and Guggenheim foundations and the National Endowment for the Arts. Her translation of poems and plays by Federico García Lorca is forthcoming from Knopf. For many years a translator for the United Nations in New York and Switzerland, she has also taught poetry at Princeton. She lives in Maryland by the Chesapeake Bay.

Arvio writes: "I was writing fast, full of emotion, when I found the words 'Buddhist' and 'nudist.' Many words in the poem spring from the sounds of those words. I loved seeing *'nudist'* become *'neurosis'* and then *'new roses,' 'Buddhist'* become *'rosebud,'* and *'bodhisattva'* find *'body'* and *'fatwa.'* I think of Rushdie when I hear the word 'fatwa': his death decree. 'Ring around the rosy' is also a reference to death, it turns out—all fall down—a song of the plague. *'Nobis pacem'* is my shorthand for *Dona nobis pacem* (Give us peace), the words of a song (from the Latin Mass) that peace activists sang around our fireplace! Beyond invoking the pleasure of peace, the poem seems to say that although lovelessness is death, love is a kind of dying. After writing the poem, I learned that the Bodhisattva is on a path toward compassion and enlightenment. Like love—when it does the right thing."

DERRICK AUSTIN was born in 1989 in Homestead, Florida. He earned his BA in English and writing from the University of Tampa and recently received his MFA in poetry from the University of Michigan. He is a Cave Canem fellow. His work has appeared in *New England*

Review, *Image: A Journal of Arts and Religion*, *Crab Orchard Review*, *The Paris-American*, and *Memorious*.

Austin writes: "The first drafts of 'Cedars of Lebanon' were written in early 2013, during my first Michigan winter. I'd lived in Florida for a decade before moving up north and, despite childhood stints in North Dakota and New Jersey, I've never acclimated to winter. I'm not made for snow boots and subzero temperatures. As a result, most of my poems exist in a perpetual summer. So, the poem is strongly influenced by my responding to my new environment: the flattening and disorienting effect of snow, icy distortions, and the alienating, seemingly perpetual darkness. In certain ways, winter is the hardest season to write poetry about—all the metaphors and images it seems to inspire move toward sleep, dormancy, isolation, and inevitably death, points of stasis. I wanted energy and movement, for desire to travel through violence and dominance and open, hopefully, into tenderness."

DESIREE BAILEY was born in Trinidad and Tobago in 1989. She grew up in Queens, New York. She studied English and African Studies at Georgetown University and is currently an MFA fiction candidate at Brown University. She has received fellowships from Princeton in Africa, the Norman Mailer Center, and the Callaloo Creative Writing Workshop. She is also a recipient of the Poets and Writers' Amy Award. She is currently the fiction editor at *Kinfolks Quarterly*.

Of "A Retrograde," Bailey writes: "This poem rose up out of the histories, experiences, and ideas to which I constantly return: the maroon communities of the Caribbean and Brazil that challenged the dominance of the plantation slavery system, the psychic trauma of a severed lineage, the historical violence that often resides in beautiful landscapes, the passing down of folklore, rites, and ways of seeing, the ocean as a mother, the ocean as a city of ancestors or as a balm.

"I pose questions in this poem: Is the liberation of the body tied to the liberation of the land? What happens to the mind when the land is warped? And vice versa? What are the consequences of cultural amnesia? How do we close the distance between the past and the present? How can we open multiple ways of seeing?"

MELISSA BARRETT has received an Ohio Arts Council Individual Excellence Award, a *Tin House* writer's scholarship, a Galway Kinnell scholarship from the Community of Writers at Squaw Valley, and a national teaching award from Building Excellent Schools. Born in Cleveland in 1983, she teaches writing at an urban middle school and lives in a century-old home in Columbus, Ohio.

Of "WFM: Allergic to Pine-Sol, Am I the Only One," Barrett writes: "An old boss of mine used to tell me stories about her daughter, who suffered from chronic congestion for most of her childhood. Years later, she discovered that she was allergic to Pine-Sol, which her mom (my boss) sprayed around the house every day. The story stuck with me because I liked the odd personal detail of knowing my boss loved Pine-Sol, and—living in the Sinus Belt and being allergic to dust—I could empathize with someone who had her fair share of runny noses. 'WFM: Allergic to Pine-Sol, Am I the Only One' was born from this story.

"It's a found poem, sourced mainly from Craigslist personal ads (though part of the title and the poem's first line come from a medical message board). I changed, added, or deleted words here and there, but the poem was pieced together almost verbatim from Craigslist. I found the writing there to be lively, honest, and genuine. Some posts were very direct, while others were more flowery—but nearly all of them hooked me with their desire to connect with another person (or *persons*, in some cases). I copied down my favorite bits, and began to edit them together.

"After mashing up the lines, I didn't think I had a poem—I considered it more of an exercise. But a few months later, I found myself still thinking about 'WFM.' The idea of recording and making permanent lines from the world's largest classifieds site (over eighty million classified ads are posted to the site each month!) drew me in. And connecting the various authors (many of whom were, um, pining after a 'missed connection') was a nice bonus."

MARK BIBBINS was born in Albany, New York, in 1968, and has lived in New York City since 1991. He is the author of three books of poems, most recently *They Don't Kill You Because They're Hungry, They Kill You Because They're Full* (Copper Canyon Press, 2014). He teaches in the graduate writing programs of The New School, where he cofounded *LIT* magazine, and Columbia University. His poems have recently appeared in *The New Yorker*, *Poetry*, *Volt*, and *The Literary Review*. He edits the poetry section of *The Awl*.

Of "Swallowed," Bibbins writes: "When Melissa Broder's last book came out, she invited a pack of us to write poems inspired by the seven deadly sins and seven heavenly virtues. I was assigned gluttony, which accounts for Ciacco's appearance—readers of Dante's *Inferno* might remember him from the third circle—although one or two other vices also banged up against the poem."

JESSAMYN BIRRER was born in Falls Church, Virginia, in 1975. She lived and worked in Idaho and Washington before moving to her current home of Klamath Falls, Oregon, where she is an autism advocate, stay-at-home parent, and technical writing instructor. Her poems have recently appeared in *Illuminations* and in *Ninth Letter*.

Of "A Scatology," Birrer writes: "Antonin Artaud said, 'Where there is a stink of shit there is a smell of being'; Salvador Dalí, that given that our 'highest mission is to spiritualize everything, it is [our] excrement in particular that needs it most.' Though I am neither French nor particularly surreal, my experience of being is no less a central concern, no less a thing both narrated and dictated by the body. I may feel as though my inward self were secret and hidden away in the closed systems of my anatomy, but in fact the body is not a closed system—in fact, we are all constantly and literally open to the world, human tunnels for food, air, and experience. We take the world in through the mouth, let it wind its way through the soft doughnut of the body, then let it go. This poem came from wanting to explore those voluntary and involuntary practices that make each of us no more and no less than any other creature. I wanted to write a love poem to being—to the anus, the alimentary canal, the body as practical and full of dirt. I wanted to revere the body."

CHANA BLOCH was born in New York City in 1940. She is professor emerita of English at Mills College, where she taught for over thirty years and directed the creative writing program. From 2007 to 2012 she served as the first poetry editor of www.persimmontree.org, an online journal of the arts by women over sixty. Her *Swimming in the Rain: New and Selected Poems, 1980–2015*, published by Autumn House Press, contains new work as well as selections from her four earlier collections— *The Secrets of the Tribe* (Sheep Meadow, 1980), *The Past Keeps Changing* (Sheep Meadow, 1992), *Mrs. Dumpty* (University of Wisconsin, 1998), and *Blood Honey* (Autumn House, 2009). She is cotranslator of the biblical *Song of Songs* (Random House, 1995; Modern Library Classic, 2006), *The Selected Poetry of Yehuda Amichai* (Harper, 1986; rev. University of California, 1996), Amichai's *Open Closed Open* (Harcourt, 2000), and *Hovering at a Low Altitude: The Collected Poetry of Dahlia Ravikovitch* (W. W. Norton, 2009). She has written a critical study, *Spelling the Word: George Herbert and the Bible* (University of California, 1985).

Of "The Joins," Bloch writes: "Two works of art and an argument—the materials for a poem. Whatever the argument was about, my husband and I had repaired the damage before I left for a month at the Djerassi Resident Artists Program in Woodside, California. On the way there, I was thinking about a ceramic cup I had seen online, a deep crimson, its surface lit by brilliant zigzags that seemed at first like a design element—a beautiful example of *kintsugi* ('golden joinery'), the art of repairing broken pottery with a lacquer resin laced with gold. This practice honors the history of a broken cup or bowl instead of attempting to disguise it; the repaired vessel is often more beautiful for having been broken.

"In the meadow at Djerassi I found myself drawn to a sculpture by a visiting artist: two conical structures, twenty feet tall, made of slender redwood branches wired together. The two stood side by side, joined at mid-height by crisscrossing branches that made a little roof overhead as you moved from one to the other. The sculptor was a German artist, Roland Mayer, who had named it, appropriately, *Dialog*. I walked in and around and between the two parts, experiencing their connection. The 'web' of branches that linked them got me thinking about the ways lovers are—and aren't—connected. Although it didn't become part of the poem itself, the time I spent with *Dialog* belongs to its prehistory, a generative experience that is stored in the body gathering energy until it can find its way into words.

"T. S. Eliot wrote that a poet's mind is 'constantly amalgamating disparate experience,' 'forming new wholes.' The Japanese art of *kintsugi* and Roland Mayer's *Dialog* joined with my memory of an argument to form a new whole, a poem celebrating the beauty of imperfection in human relationships as in art."

EMMA BOLDEN was born in Birmingham, Alabama, in 1980. She graduated from Sarah Lawrence College and received her MFA from the University of North Carolina at Wilmington. She is the author of two full-length collections of poetry: *Maleficae* (GenPop Books, 2013) and *medi(t)ations* (Noctuary Press, 2015). She has written four chapbooks of poetry: *How to Recognize a Lady* (part of *Edge by Edge*, Toadlily Press, 2007); *The Mariner's Wife* (Finishing Line Press, 2008); *The Sad Epistles* (Dancing Girl Press, 2008); and *This Is Our Hollywood* (in *The Chapbook*, 2013). She has also written a nonfiction chapbook, *Geography V* (Winged City Press, 2014).

Of "House Is an Enigma," Bolden writes: "If language is the house in which we all dwell, this poem provided me with a key. I wrote it in the midst of a situation that I'd been told, in so many ways, that I wasn't supposed to talk about. So let me talk about it here, and plainly, and publicly, for the first time: I was about to have a total hysterectomy. For twenty-some years, I'd struggled with endometriosis and a host of other so-called 'female problems' so rarely spoken about, publicly or privately, that they're known as silent epidemics. I was single and childless and thirty-two years old. I was furiously silent and furious with silence. I was also furious with language. I faced the biggest decision of my life and even the physician charged with helping me to make this decision spoke in metaphors, which invariably referenced houses. 'I don't think,' he would say, 'that your womb could viably house a fetus.' On a long and rambling drive through long and rambling rural Georgia, I noticed that I'd started to notice houses: row after row of them, all settling into their foundations with increasingly unsettled faces. After passing one particularly angry house, it occurred to me that perhaps the house was every bit as angry as I was with the metaphor my doctor used to talk about my situation. I began to write a poem in which the house talked about its frustrations with language and, through its doors, I began to settle my own frustrations and dwell more comfortably—and honestly—in the house that is my body."

DEXTER L. BOOTH was born in Richmond, Virginia, in 1986. He is the author of *Scratching the Ghost* (Graywolf Press, 2013), which won the 2012 Cave Canem Poetry Prize and was selected by Major Jackson. His poems appear in *Blackbird, The Southeast Review, Ostrich Review, Grist, Willow Springs*, and *Virginia Quarterly Review*. He is currently a PhD candidate at the University of Southern California.

Of "Prayer at 3 a.m.," Booth writes: "Ultimately, our bodies fail us. Our voices fail us. Words fail us, too, but fortunately they hold up better and far longer than bodies do. Faith and hope (pick your brand: Religion, Humanity, Family . . .) are intangible, yet they're two of the most vital things we can possess as humans. Youth can be a type of blindness, and that blindness can be sacred.

"Amendment: Everything is sacred. Everything is sacred. Even death."

CATHERINE BOWMAN was born on November 26, 1957, in El Paso, Texas. She is the author of *1-800-HOT-RIBS* (Gibbs Smith, 1993), *Rock Farm* (Gibbs Smith, 1996), *Notarikon* (Four Way Books, 2006), *The Plath Cabinet* (Four Way Books, 2009), and *Can I Finish, Please?* (Four Way Books, 2016). She has edited *Word of Mouth, Poems Featured on NPR's All Things Considered.* She lives on a farm in Bloomington, Indiana, and teaches at Indiana University.

Bowman writes: "I was thinking about the word 'makeshift,' imagining what it means to 'make do' or 'shift making' with the tools at hand—the imagination—within states of loss, abandonment, exile, environmental destruction, oil spills, etc.—the makeshift father, the makeshift mother, the makeshift grave, the makeshift holy city. The first lines in the poem came out of seeing photos of shorebirds and waterfowl, the laughing gull and royal tern covered in oil following the Gulf oil disaster. In what ways is the imagination resilient, generative, and/or destructive? I guess that is what the chiastic structure revealed for me, though I am not really sure. I am intrigued by the image of a fire ladder. I was working on the poem and had written several lines and was feeling kind of stuck. I was thinking about the poem when I went to bed and hoped some solution would come up while sleeping. That night I had a dream in which a sideways wooden X appeared. That's how the chiastic structure emerged. The poem ends with 'string pieces for two': music?—hopeful, I think."

RACHAEL BRIGGS was born in Syracuse, New York, in 1984, but has lived for the last eight years in Australia. She is an associate professor in philosophy at the University of Queensland, and a research associate at the Australian National University. Her first collection of poems, *Free Logic*, was published in 2013 by University of Queensland Press.

Briggs writes: "'in the hall of the ruby-throated warbler' is a love poem. When I wrote it, I followed the sounds and the feelings, and let the ideas follow. It's in Sapphic meter (or the English translation of Sapphic meter), which I feel is one of the most beautiful rhythmic devices I can command. Sapphic meter is also appropriate for a love poem addressed to a woman, by a woman. I've been writing Sapphic sonnets ever since a friend, commenting on another of my Sapphic love poems, complained that the last two lines weren't pulling their weight. First I thought, 'I can't cut the second half of a stanza! That's against the formal rules!' Then I thought, 'Says who?'"

JERICHO BROWN has received a Whiting Writers Award and fellowships from the Radcliffe Institute for Advanced Study at Harvard University and the National Endowment for the Arts. His poems have appeared in *The New Republic*, *The New Yorker*, and *The Best American Poetry*. His first book, *Please* (New Issues, 2008), won the American Book Award, and his second book, *The New Testament* (Copper Canyon, 2014), was named one of the best books of the year by *Library Journal* and the Academy of American Poets. He is an assistant professor in the creative writing program at Emory University in Atlanta.

Brown writes: "Can a single poem be: surreal, personal, about a 'we' just as much as it is about an 'I,' political, and interested in pop culture and current events? I wrote 'Homeland' thinking about Henry Louis Gates and Barack Obama and what it means to be a very lonely citizen in a country that doesn't want your citizenship."

RAFAEL CAMPO, MA, MD, DLitt, was born in Dover, New Jersey, in 1964, and teaches and practices internal medicine at Harvard Medical School and Beth Israel Deaconess Medical Center in Boston. He is on the faculty of Lesley University's creative writing MFA program. He has received a Guggenheim Fellowship, a National Poetry Series award, and a Lambda Literary Award for his poetry. His third collection of poetry, *Diva* (Duke University Press, 2000), was a finalist for the National Book Critics Circle Award, and *The Enemy* (DUP, 2007) won the Sheila Motton Book Award from the New England Poetry Club. In 2009, he received the Nicholas E. Davies Memorial Scholar Award from the American College of Physicians, for outstanding humanism in medicine; he has also won the Hippocrates Open International Prize for original verse that addresses a medical theme. *Alternative Medicine* (DUP, 2013), his newest book, has recently been the subject of stories on *PBS NewsHour* and the CBC's *Sunday Edition* radio show.

Campo writes: "My intent in the poem was to reflect on the tension between 'fact' and 'truth' in the distinct kinds of stories we tell about ourselves when we are ill. As a physician, I am trained to value only the factual data pertaining to a patient's disease: what the potassium level is, how many lymph nodes are enlarged on the CT scan, which antiretroviral medication causes what side effect. Yet the poet in me always yearns to understand the human truths of our experience of illness, such as what does it mean when we say 'the pain is like a cold wind blowing on my face' or 'silence equals death.' Too often in medicine, we doctors use our relentless focus on fact and our steely 'medicalese' as means of distancing ourselves from the people under our care, to make it easier for us to get through our endless work; I believe that the empathy that arises from a more truthful engagement with illness, one that embraces diverse ways of knowing about suffering and the richly metaphoric language those under our care use to describe it, can actually make us better healers. Thus when I saw the newspaper headline 'Doctors Lie, May Hide Mistakes,' I felt acutely the irony in how the physician's usual dispassionate, don't-tell-me-what-you-feel stance, which does contribute to poorer outcomes for patients, can also lead to misrepresenting the very facts we so slavishly pursue. The poem, then, becomes the indelible medium for more deeply wondering at when our bodies betray us, and things go terribly wrong; perhaps it is all the more necessary when there is no new analgesic that is more effective for the chronic pain, or the tumor is inoperable. I do not mean to say that fact and truth cannot coexist in addressing illness; on the contrary, they are utterly complementary, and the narrative of illness that entails both is the closest we can get to offering meaningful hope to the afflicted. In the end, it is our shared vulnerability, our imperfections and our frailty, our inability (no matter how much information we memorize or statistics we calculate) to escape our mortality, that makes us all human."

JULIE CARR was born in Cambridge, Massachusetts, in 1966. She is the author of six books of poetry, including *100 Notes on Violence* (Ahsahta, 2010), *Sarah—Of Fragments and Lines* (Coffee House, 2010), *RAG* (Omnidawn, 2014), and *Think Tank* (Solid Objects, 2015). She is also the author of *Surface Tension: Ruptural Time and the Poetics of Desire in Late Victorian Poetry* (Dalkey Archive, 2013), and coeditor of *Active Romanticism: The Radical Impulse in Nineteenth-Century and Contemporary Poetic Practice* (Alabama UP, 2015). Her cotranslations of Apollinaire and contemporary French poet Leslie Kaplan have been published in *Denver Quarterly* and *Kenyon Review*, and a chapbook of selections from Kaplan's *Excess— The Factory* has been released by Commune Editions. A 2011–2012 NEA fellow, she is an associate professor at the University of Colorado in Boulder, where she teaches in the MFA creative writing program and the Intermedia Arts Writing and Performance PhD program. She regularly collaborates with the dance artist K. J. Holmes. She lives in Denver and helps to run Counterpath Press and Counterpath Gallery.

Carr writes: "'A fourteen-line poem on sex' is one of many fourteen-line poems I've been writing as interludes in a long project called *Real Life: An Installation*. They are an experiment in propulsion, disjunction, and radical enjambment. In this one, for the first and perhaps last time, I pun on my name. The portion of I-40, the 'Music Highway,' that runs from Nashville to Asheville passes through Knoxville and the foothills of the Crab Orchard Mountains. I probably ran out of gas near the Pigeon River Gorge. I hiked across the median, down a grassy slope, and across another highway to find a gas station. A kind gentleman drove me back to the car with a plastic jug of gas between my feet."

CHEN CHEN was born in Xiamen, China, in 1989. He received his MFA in poetry from Syracuse University in spring 2015. A Kundiman Fellow, he has published his work in *Poetry*, *The Massachusetts Review*, *DIAGRAM*, and *Crab Orchard Review*. He was a finalist for *Narrative*'s 30 Below Contest and won second place in the Joy Harjo Poetry Prizes from *Cutthroat: A Journal of the Arts*. For more information, visit chenchenwrites.com.

Of "for i will do/undo what was done/undone to me," Chen writes: "I spent three years in Syracuse, New York, pursuing an MFA in poetry. It snowed a lot. I learned about lake effect and Wallace Stevens's 'The Snow Man' and how to walk to campus without slipping and breaking an arm. People in the program said, 'Don't write a Syracuse snow poem' and 'You're going to write a Syracuse snow poem eventually.' This is the Syracuse snow poem I could not help writing. I'm not sure if it is an elegy or an ode. Either way, it is a shivery love letter to the weathers and mysteries of a place that has given me so much."

SUSANNA CHILDRESS was born in 1978 in La Mirada, California, and, after living overseas, grew up in the near-Appalachia of southern Indiana. She has also spent time in Austin, where she received a master's from the University of Texas; Tallahassee, where she received a PhD from Florida State; Oklahoma City, where she received a husband; Valparaiso, Indiana, where she held a Lilly postdoctoral fellowship in the Arts and Humanities; and now Holland, Michigan, where she teaches creative writing at Hope College. She is the author of *Jagged with Love* (University of Wisconsin Press, 2005) and *Entering the House of Awe* (New Issues Poetry & Prose, 2011). She is an associate editor of *32 Poems*, works with the Jack Ridl Visiting Writers Series, publishes short fiction and creative nonfiction, and constitutes, along with Joshua Banner, the music group Ordinary Neighbors, whose full-length debut, *The Necessary Dark*, is based on her writing.

Of "Careful, I Just Won a Prize at the Fair," Childress writes: "The date on the first draft of this poem, twice as long as the end result, indicates that I was six months pregnant with our second child, so I'm guessing that, between hyperemesis gravidarum (all-day morning sickness to the point of grave danger) and hypersomnia (a cousin to narcolepsy—untreatable during pregnancy), I inhabited generous grounds for my anger and exhaustion and pathos. Still, when I read the poem now, I sense a straddling: I had a foot in two hemispheres. Inside a marriage, a home, a womb: love does nothing and everything and nourishes and depletes and worms its way into grand moments as well as the frivolous and diurnal. How can we imagine love accomplishes *anything*. How can we go a full minute without it. What are we (each) in its cuffs if not barreling, broken, majestic."

Yɪ-Fᴇɴ Cʜᴏᴜ is the pen name of Michael Derrick Hudson, who was born in Wabash, Indiana, in 1963. He currently lives in Fort Wayne, Indiana, where he works for the Allen County Public Library in the Genealogy Center. A portfolio of five of his poems was recently named cowinner of the 2014 Manchester Poetry Prize. His poems have won *The Madison Review* 2009 Phyllis Smart Young Prize, *River Styx* 2009 International Poetry Contest, and the 2010 and 2013 *New Ohio Review* contests. In addition to *Prairie Schooner*, his poems have appeared in various journals, including *Boulevard, Columbia, Fugue, The Georgia Review, Gulf Coast, The Iowa Review, New Letters, New Orleans Review, Northwest Review, Prick of the Spindle, Washington Square,* and *West Branch.*

He writes: "There is a very short answer for my use of a nom de plume: after a poem of mine has been rejected a multitude of times under my real name, I put Yi-Fen's name on it and send it out again. As a strategy for 'placing' poems this has been quite successful for me. The poem in question, 'The Bees, the Flowers, Jesus, Ancient Tigers, Poseidon, Adam and Eve,' was rejected under my real name forty (40) times before I sent it out as Yi-Fen Chou (I keep detailed submission records). As Yi-Fen the poem was rejected nine (9) times before *Prairie Schooner* took it. If indeed this is one of the best American poems of 2015, it took quite a bit of effort to get it into print, but I'm nothing if not persistent.

"I realize that this isn't a very 'artistic' explanation for using a pseudonym. Years ago I did briefly consider trying to make Yi-Fen into a 'persona' or 'heteronym' à la Fernando Pessoa, but nothing ever came of it.

"'The Bees, the Flowers, Jesus, Ancient Tigers, Poseidon, Adam and Eve' is made up of bungled or half-bungled history, botany, entomology, mythology, and theology. That engineers or scientists once insisted that bumblebees can't really fly is false, according to Snopes.com. Years ago I read that some of the plants found growing on the ruins of the Colosseum in Rome are otherwise found only in Africa or the Near East, brought in with (and excreted by) the exotic animals brought to be slaughtered in the arena. This might be true, but even so it is more likely rhinoceroses or giraffes pooped the seeds, but tiger poop seemed more apt and funnier to me (I also had T. S. Eliot's 'Christ the tiger' from 'Gerontion' vaguely in mind). 'Jesus wept' is the King James Bible verse everybody knows, since it is the shortest (John 11:35), and I kept it intact here. But I don't think Poseidon ever had anything to do with Philomel, a myth I also filched from Eliot (who got her from Ovid, according to Wikipedia). The jellyfish I got from visits to Cocoa Beach, Florida, where they sometimes wash up by the score and I always worry about stepping on them.

"The result I was hoping for with all this bungling (as much as poems have results) was to suggest Original Sin, or at least that *echt*-human feeling of being *wrong* most of the time. And how getting things wrong goes back a long, long time for us. I wasn't trying to blame this mess on Eve."

ERICA DAWSON was born in Columbia, Maryland, in 1979. Her first collection of poems, *Big-Eyed Afraid*, won the 2006 Anthony Hecht Poetry Prize and was published by Waywiser Press in 2007. Measure Press published her second collection, *The Small Blades Hurt*, in 2014. Her work has appeared twice in *The Best American Poetry*. She is an assistant professor of English and writing at the University of Tampa.

Of "Slow-Wave Sleep with a Fairy Tale," Dawson writes: "One Sunday I picked up an old copy of *Grimm's Fairy Tales*, read 'Little Briar Rose' three times, and remembered how, as a child, I put myself in princess' shoes. I slept for a hundred years. I woke to a prince. As an adult, I saw myself as a new character in the story, but still regular Erica. Everything was magical except for me.

"When I started the sonnet, the context of a dream made sense, especially a dream during slow-wave sleep where there's no rapid eye movement but sometimes parasomnias like sleepwalking or night terrors. I liked the idea of a kind of unconscious agency—moving through a world you're not quite part of as you're crashing through it.

"The other day I shaved Rapunzel's head."

DANIELLE DETIBERUS was born in Connecticut in 1980. She has lived all along the East Coast of the United States—from Boston, Massachusetts, to Asheville, North Carolina, and a few places in between. She now lives and teaches in Charleston, South Carolina, where she serves as the program chair for the Poetry Society of South Carolina. Her work has appeared in *Arts and Letters*, *The Southeast Review*, *Spoon River Poetry Review*, and *Tar River Poetry*.

Of "In a Black Tank Top," DeTiberus writes: "In my manuscript,

I write a lot about love—about its complexities, about how one can never fully know one's beloved. On the day I wrote the first draft of this poem, I was thinking about how much desire propels and sustains a long-term relationship, which is mired in the domestic, the banal. The body can have so much power over the mind, and the first time we're truly aware of this is during puberty. High school, then, is a fiery experiment: a contained space with pulsing sparks, dreaming about and trying to ignite with one another. I wanted to marry that juvenile, twitterpated longing with a more mature, knowing voice. This poem makes me laugh—and blush; I think that it's sexy precisely because it approaches sex from the perspective of someone who is just discovering her sexuality. It's also, of course, cheeky because it's a concrete poem. That idea occurred to me only after several drafts, and it felt like a nod to the days I'd dot my i's with hearts. Shaping it into a visual poem was an attempt to re-create the immediacy of the gaze, which can be at once tender and dominant. My hope is that this poem looks back at the reader with a wink, like a lover, coy and unabashed."

NATALIE DIAZ was born and raised in the Fort Mojave Indian Village in Needles, California, on the banks of the Colorado River. She is Mojave and an enrolled member of the Gila River Indian Tribe. Her first poetry collection, *When My Brother Was an Aztec*, was published by Copper Canyon Press. She is a 2012 Lannan Literary Fellow and a 2012 Native Arts Council Foundation Artist Fellow. In 2014, she was awarded a Bread Loaf Fellowship, as well as the Holmes National Poetry Prize from Princeton University and a U.S. Artists Ford Fellowship. Diaz teaches at the Institute of American Indian Arts Low Rez MFA program and lives in Mohave Valley, Arizona, where she directs the Fort Mojave Language Recovery Program, working with the last remaining speakers at Fort Mojave to teach and revitalize the Mojave language.

Of "It Was the Animals," Diaz writes: "Sometimes a god sends a storm or flood and it is a type of love. We gather up all the beasts, including ourselves, including our brothers, because we were built like other animals, with an instinct to *survive*. Maybe it is more than an instinct, maybe it is *surviving* that we do as a rule, and *living* is what is a luckiness when we manage to do it well enough to call it a celebration, to call it *life*. My love for my brother is both the flood and the ark. It is what makes me want to teach him the error of his ways but also what makes me want to hold him as we ride out whatever storm is battering us. He has his animals and I have mine. They hollow us. They make us dark inside. They split us open on the rocks. At the end of it all everything has changed—the land, the sky, the rivers, the sea—but what doesn't change is that we are brother and sister. What never changes is love."

DENISE DUHAMEL was born in Providence, Rhode Island, in 1961. *Blowout* (University of Pittsburgh Press, 2013), her most recent book of poems, was a finalist for the National Book Critics Circle Award and winner of a 2014 Paterson Poetry Prize. Her other books include *Ka-Ching!* (Pittsburgh, 2009), *Two and Two* (Pittsburgh, 2005), *Queen for a Day: Selected and New Poems* (Pittsburgh, 2001), *The Star-Spangled Banner* (winner of the Crab Orchard Award; Southern Illinois University Press, 1999), and *Kinky* (Orchises Press, 1997). She has received fellowships from the Guggenheim Foundation and the National Endowment for the Arts. The guest editor of *The Best American Poetry 2013*, she is a professor at Florida International University in Miami.

Of "Fornicating," Duhamel writes: "In July 2012 I had the good fortune to be in Lisbon with the Disquiet Program. I went to hear a lecture by Richard Zenith about the history of Portuguese verse. He ended with a few poems by contemporary poet Adília Lopes, and I was immediately hooked. I sensed in her work urgency and hilarity and have since sought out her poems that are translated into English. The lines I quote are from Lopes's 'Weather Report.' You can read some of her work at www.poetryinternationalweb.net."

THOMAS SAYERS ELLIS was born on October 5, 1963, and attended Paul Laurence Dunbar High School in Washington, D.C. He earned his MFA at Brown University under the sharp, tough, and eye-opening tutelage of poet Michael S. Harper. He cofounded the Dark Room Collective in 1988. He is a photographer, poet, and professor, and his poems have appeared in *Callaloo*, *Poetry*, *The Paris Review*, *Pluck!*, *The Nation*, *Tin House*, and *Transition*. His photographs have appeared on numerous book covers. He has recently been a visiting writer at the University of San Francisco, Wesleyan University, Howard University, and the University of Montana. He is the author of *The Maverick Room* (2005) and *Skin, Inc.: Identity Repair Poems* (2010). In 2014, he cofounded (with saxophonist James Brandon Lewis) Heroes Are Gang Leaders, an Amiri Baraka tribute band of poets and musicians.

Ellis writes: " 'Vernacular Owl' was written, mostly, in bed in San Francisco and edited while crossing America numerous times on the California Zephyr (Amtrak). I was paid $2,230 for the publication of it in *Poetry* magazine, $250 for the recording of the poem for the Poetry Foundation's podcast; and $500 more, by the Poetry Foundation, when the poem received the Salmon O. Levinson Prize. The appearance of 'Vernacular Owl' in this anthology will add $100, bringing the total to $3,080, all of which was used to fund the three recording sessions, engineering and mixing fees for the project Heroes Are Gang Leaders/ The Amiri Baraka Sessions. 'Vernacular Owl' is not an elegy. The poem attempts to express the transformation of nonmaterial flight."

EMILY KENDAL FREY was born in McLean, Virginia, in 1976. She is the author of several chapbooks and chapbook collaborations, including *Frances*, *Airport*, *Baguette*, and *The New Planet*. *The Grief Performance*, her first full-length collection, won the Norma Farber First Book Award from the Poetry Society of America in 2012. *Sorrow Arrow*, her second collection, was published by Octopus Books in 2014.

JAMES GALVIN was born in Chicago in 1951 and raised in Northern Colorado. His first four books are collected in *Resurrection Update*, published by Copper Canyon Press. Also published by Copper Canyon are *X* and *As Is*. He is the author of two prose works, *The Meadow* and *Fencing the Sky*, published by Henry Holt. He teaches at the Iowa Writers' Workshop.

Of "On the Sadness of Wedding Dresses," Galvin writes: "W. B. Yeats wrote, 'How but in custom and in ceremony / Are innocence and beauty born?' Good question. I saw a wedding dress on display at Goodwill and it got me thinking. As a poet, I could identify with that dress, and also with all the dresses that, after so much care and deliberation, are worn once, then trapped in darkness, alone. My poem is a tracery of my thinking and feeling about the situation of wedding dresses."

MADELYN GARNER was born in Denver, Colorado, in 1937. A graduate of the University of Denver (BA) and Mills College (MEd), she is a retired public school administrator and instructor of English. She has received the Colorado Governor's Award for Excellence in the Arts and Humanities for encouraging incorporation of the arts into school programs. Named a Leo Love Merit Scholar at the Taos Summer Writers' Conference, she was awarded an Aspen Writers' Foundation's Annual Writing Retreat scholarship. In 2010, she won the Jackson Hole Writers Conference Poetry Prize. With coeditor Andrea L. Watson, she published the anthology *Collecting Life: Poets on Objects Known and Imagined* (3: A Taos Press, 2013).

Garner writes: "'The Garden in August' began with the powerful image of an older neighbor in her garden and then developed into a semibiographical account of my sister's fatal battle with Alzheimer's. As the poem progressed, I grew interested in what my neighbor might have done the day after I saw her, and in the process I found myself viewing her as a representative figure for those who choose to live life with dogged persistence and admirable willpower no matter how challenging. I often write about them: the elderly world adventurer planning yet another trip (next year, maybe Cuba?); the survivor of a near-death experience now healthy enough to walk her beloved Airedale several miles daily; my sister.

"Soon it will be spring in the Rocky Mountains, and once more I will breakfast on the back patio in my own well-worn robe so I might enjoy the exuberance of parrot tulips planted in late October. Under hand there will be a growing nursery list of annuals to be purchased for this year's garden, *Ageratum houstonianum* through *Zinnia elegans*, and a folder with multiple drafts of the poem I am working on at the moment. Later in the day, I will probably search for my favorite floppy-brimmed hat and check the garden hoses for weathering, perhaps even clean up the yard. I will do this, as the poem reminds me, because I am alive."

AMY GERSTLER was born in San Diego, California, in 1956. She teaches at the University of California at Irvine. Her books of poems include *Dearest Creature* (Penguin, 2009), *Ghost Girl* (Penguin, 2004), and *Medicine* (Penguin, 2000). A new book of poems entitled *Scattered at Sea* came out from Penguin in June 2015. She was the guest editor of *The Best American Poetry 2010*.

Of "Rhinencephalon," Gerstler writes: "This poem came about due to a confluence of reading about refugees (some of whom get separated from their loved ones and families in the process of fleeing conflict zones and trying to emigrate to safety), thinking about various other types of displacement and homelessness that people suffer, and an urge to write a kind of love poem. Somewhere in the mix is also the influence of reading and thinking about the role of smell in love and attraction. The rhinencephalon is a part of an animal's brain—not terribly well developed in humans, apparently—that contains structures having to do with the sense of smell. I was thinking with envy of the fact that certain other animals with more sophisticated olfactory capabilities can recognize each other by smell."

Louise Glück was born in New York City in 1943. Her most recent books of poetry, both from Farrar, Straus and Giroux, are *Faithful and Virtuous Night*, which received a 2014 National Book Award, and *Poems 1962–2012*. A former United States Poet Laureate, she has won a National Book Critics Circle Award and a Pulitzer Prize. She teaches at Yale University and Boston University, and was the 2014–2015 Mohr Writer in Residence at Stanford University. She was the guest editor of *The Best American Poetry 1993*.

R. S. (Sam) Gwynn was born in Leaksville (now Eden), North Carolina, in 1948. After attending Davidson College, he entered the graduate program at the University of Arkansas, where he earned his MFA. Since 1976, he has taught at Lamar University, where he is poet-in-residence and University Professor of English. His first two collections were chapbooks, *Bearing & Distance* (1977) and *The Narcissiad* (1980). These were followed by *The Drive-In* (1986) and *No Word of Farewell: New and Selected Poems 1970–2000*. His new collection is *Dogwatch* (2014) from Measure Press. His criticism appears regularly in *The Hudson Review*, and he is editor of the Pocket Anthology Series from Pearson-Longman. He lives in Beaumont, Texas, with his wife, Donna. They have three sons and seven grandchildren.

Gwynn writes: "The origin of 'Looney Tunes' is a little unusual. Several years ago, a friend, an English poet, sent me a page that reprinted the winner and finalists of a *TLS* poetry competition, mentioning that both the winner and the first runner-up were friends of hers. I liked both poems, but 'The Examiners' by John Whitworth (it's easy enough to find the poem online) struck me as superior to the winner. I asked her to put me in touch with John, and after a few emails we both, I think, realized a match made in poets' heaven (Limbo?). We were both of an age and, though separated by the pond, enjoyed doing the same sorts of things with verse. Quickly after this, I wrote 'Looney Tunes' (originally titled 'Dirge') as an homage to John, to whom it is dedicated. Knowing John's poems freed me up to write verse in dipodic meters (beloved by Kipling and Gilbert) and to use rhyme as audaciously as I dared. I hope that those who enjoy this bit of metrical madness will look up and read Whitworth's poems; he is little known in the United States for the usual reasons. I was proud to host him at Lamar University for his first U.S. visit (even if it was only to southeast Texas), to take him to an Astros game (he is a cricket fanatic), and to let him give my students and many others unforgettable classroom performances and a public reading. A very good reading of 'Looney Tunes' (with appropriate visuals) can be found on YouTube at the archive of the great 'Tom O'Bedlam,' who has given a remarkable public voice to so many poems by me and others. For his readings, see htps://www.youtube.com/user/SpokenVerse."

MEREDITH HASEMANN lives in East Hampton, New York. When she's not teaching eighth-grade English, you might find her searching for beach glass, carving and burning driftwood, or playing guitar and bass for the North Branch All Stars. Although right now she lives full-time in the Hamptons, her heart is in the Green Mountains of Vermont, where she will return one day. She is seeking a publisher for her first book of poetry. Her young adult novels are represented by the Nancy Gallt Literary Agency.

Of "Thumbs," Hasemann writes: "This poem began to write itself on a shared hike in Vermont. Although the conversation centered upon hydroponic tomatoes, my background brain was buzzing with the chaos of my unnecessarily dramatic and drawn-out divorce and a host of other facts, concerns, and scraps of brain matter. A stacked stone wall near the apple orchard on North Branch Road led me to marvel at how each of these stones added precariously together to create a new whole, and how they just happened to fit. I tried to write 'Thumbs' like that stone wall, stacking my concerns one on top of the next to see if I could climb onto the construction and actually see anything beyond. For me, 'Thumbs' represents freedom. It's about allowing a poem to exist on many planes and to be free to go where it wants.

"I often wonder about how past and present fit together and how memory and thought work. We have so many layers crammed inside our brain, how is it at all possible to express anything at all? This poem was my attempt to allow the competing voices and experiences in my head to inform each other, instead of stifling them. It's about accepting a number of story lines and how they converge."

TERRANCE HAYES was born in Columbia, South Carolina, in 1971. He is the author of *How to Be Drawn* (Penguin, 2015). His other books are *Lighthead* (Penguin, 2010), *Wind in a Box* (Penguin, 2006), *Hip Logic* (Penguin, 2002), and *Muscular Music* (Tia Chucha Press, 1999). He has won a 2010 National Book Award and a 2014 MacArthur Fellowship. He teaches at the University of Pittsburgh. He was the guest editor of *The Best American Poetry 2014*.

Hayes writes: "'Antebellum House Party' owes its life to a project by Ray McManus, a fellow South Carolina–born poet, who invited me to write a poem for an anthology he was editing, *Found Anew: New Writing Inspired by the South Caroliniana Library Digital Collections*. I don't typically write poems by request, but after I came across an especially intriguing photograph (digital.tcl.sc.edu/cdm/singleitem/collection/bcp/id/27/rec/8), the poem came into focus. I hope it speaks for itself. Meanwhile, just recently a friend who'd read the poem forwarded a quote from Lyndon Johnson to his African American chauffer, Robert Parker: 'Just pretend you're a goddamn piece of furniture.' The context for this quote awaits you in cyberspace."

REBECCA HAZELTON was born in Richmond, Virginia, in 1978. She is the author of *Fair Copy* (Ohio State University Press, 2011) and *Vow* (Cleveland State University Press, 2013).

Hazelton writes: "I wrote 'My Husband' because there is so much attention given to the early stages of love, and so little given to long-term relationships (unless, of course, they are going badly). I wanted to write a poem that celebrated the delight and sensuality of the quotidian."

JANE HIRSHFIELD (born New York City, 1953) is the author of eight books of poetry, including the newly published *The Beauty* (Knopf, 2015), and two books of essays, *Nine Gates: Entering the Mind of Poetry* (HarperCollins, 1997) and the newly published *Ten Windows: How Great Poems Transform the World* (Knopf, 2015). She has also edited and cotranslated four books presenting the work of world poets from the past. She has won fellowships from the Guggenheim and Rockefeller foundations, the NEA, and the Academy of American Poets. Her work appears in seven previous editions of *The Best American Poetry* and the 25th anniversary *Best of the Best American Poetry*. She is a chancellor of the Academy of American Poets.

Of "A Common Cold," Hirshfield writes: "It will not surprise any reader to learn that I started this poem during the long (far more than eight days) course of the cold it describes. I was staying at the Civitella Ranieri in Umbria—where almost all the other residents caught the same cold. No remedy seemed to help. One day, still sick, I joined a group going to see a number of nearby Piero della Francesca paintings, including the famous *Madonna del Parto*, who stands, heavy with child, between drawn-back curtains. Alone with the painting for a few unexpected minutes, I found sudden, silent tears streaming down my face.

"Over the next days, I began to think about colds, about their independent lives from their own point of view, about how they must possess a kind of immortality, mutating perhaps but meanwhile unceasingly traveling from one person to another, one circumstance to another, one country to another, one decade, century, millennium, to another. This poem is in part the Baedeker Guide a cold virus might write (though every place mentioned is somewhere I have been, on poetry-related travels that often do seem to lead to colds—or perhaps to the one, ever-changing cold I keep meeting again wherever I go). A cold is in some ways not unlike a work of art: it inhabits each of us acutely but differently, and is passed from person to person because we are incapable of resisting its passage through us. There is also the impeccably democratic solidarity of colds to be admired: colds do not care if they are in the nose of a dictator or of a four-year-old, in the confines of a prison cell or the presence of a painting so transcendent it conquers all possibilities of separation—whether belief, time, culture, even the exhausted misery of many nights' coughing. For those moments, there was remedy after all. But perhaps the virus was also—in the phrase we sometimes use to describe the condition of being riveted—stopped cold in its tracks by Piero della Francesca's painting."

BETHANY SCHULTZ HURST was born in Parker, Colorado, in 1978. She is currently an assistant professor of English at Idaho State University. Her first book of poems, *Miss Lost Nation* (Anhinga, 2014), won the Robert Dana–Anhinga Prize for Poetry.

Of *"Crisis on Infinite Earths*, Issues 1–12," Hurst writes: "In this poem, I was interested in exploring public vs. private stances in mourning. What's the difference between paying respects and producing a self-centered display? What separates necessary attention to a disaster from morbid curiosity or rubbernecking? The poem's speaker struggles to find those boundaries, as well as the appropriate emotional response for personal 'disasters.'

"The first section, about wanting to be at Comic Con, came from a fragment of a dream, and for the speaker, superheroes seemed the answer: these would be the invulnerable figures to counter the speaker's confusion. But it turns out that superheroes, who juggle saving the world with maintaining an unassuming secret identity, are also all about the struggle between private and public persona. Reboots and multiple authorship have created confusion for superhero identities. It's intriguing that maybe these characters endure because of their fundamental inconsistencies."

SAEED JONES's debut poetry collection, *Prelude to Bruise* (Coffee House Press), won the 2015 Stonewall Book Award/Barbara Gittings Literature Award and was a finalist for the 2015 National Book Critics Circle Award. He has received fellowships from Cave Canem and Queer/Art/Mentorship.

Jones writes: "'Body & Kentucky Bourbon' is loosely based on a brief relationship I had with a man I desired but did not truly understand or love. I didn't realize just how much we had been strangers to one another until well after the relationship ended. And I began to wonder if, in fact, this intimate strangeness is perhaps more common than one would expect. I wanted to write a poem that would force me—every time I read it—to reflect on everything I did not and could not know about him as a kind of penance for not having the presence of mind to just ask him when we were still a part of each other's life."

JOAN NAVIYUK KANE was born in Anchorage, Alaska, in 1977. She teaches at the low-residency MFA program in creative writing at the Institute of American Indian Arts. Inupiaq with family from King Island and Mary's Igloo, Alaska, she raises her young sons in Anchorage. A graduate of Harvard College and the School of the Arts at Columbia University, she is the author of *The Cormorant Hunter's Wife* (published in 2009 by NorthShore Press Alaska and brought back into print in 2012 by the University of Alaska Press) and *Hyperboreal* (University of Pittsburgh Press, 2013). She has received a Whiting Writers' Award, the AWP Donald Hall Prize in Poetry, an American Book Award, the Alaska Literary Award, an artist fellowship from the Rasmuson Foundation, a fellowship from the Native Arts and Cultures Foundation, and the United States Artists Creative Vision award.

Of "Exhibits from the Dark Museum," Kane writes: "I was fortunate to work closely with the elders committee of Sitnasuak Native Corporation in Nome, Alaska, on several years of Inupiaq language projects and subsistence calendars. The meetings never passed without hours of stories about Nome, our home villages, or places far distant. The poem here arose after one of these meetings, when I'd returned to Anchorage on the flight from Nome that travels north through the subarctic before turning south to Anchorage. One of the elders had been cleaning out old buildings in Nome, with the contents of the buildings dating from Nome's gold rush, and talking about the many hauntings and layers of history that populate both the town and our memories of all the change we've seen and continue to see in Alaska. I arrived in Anchorage and couldn't sleep, troubled by images and stories of disturbance, feeling unsettled. I got up to write the poem as my husband and children slept."

LAURA KASISCHKE was born in Lake Charles, Louisiana, in 1961. She has published eight collections of poetry, most recently *The Infinitesimals* (Copper Canyon, 2014), as well as eight novels. She has received the National Book Critics Circle Award. She lives in Chelsea, Michigan, and teaches at the University of Michigan.

Of "For the Young Woman I Saw Hit by a Car While Riding Her Bike," Kasischke writes: "The poem contains the story of this minor accident, just as it happened, along with my overreaction to it, which brought in an ambulance and drew a crowd. The end of the poem is, I suppose, my excuse for that overreaction. Witnessing it threw me back to another time and place—where part of me resides permanently, I guess, and from which, I think, all these years later, I relive the other experience in every fender bender I see, and every time a loved one gets the flu or comes home an hour late, all that. I'm not sure I'd made this connection so clearly before I wrote this poem—not that it will change anything, but at least I got a poem out of it."

Born in Brooklyn, New York, and raised in Altadena, California, DOUGLAS KEARNEY lives with his family in California's Santa Clarita Valley. He teaches in the BFA in critical studies and the MFA in creative writing at CalArts, where he received his MFA in writing (2004). His third poetry collection, *Patter* (Red Hen Press, 2014), examines miscarriage, infertility, and parenthood. His second book, *The Black Automaton* (Fence Books, 2009), was a National Poetry Series selection. He has received residencies or fellowships from Cave Canem and the Rauschenberg Foundation. Two of his operas, *Sucktion* and *Crescent City*, have received grants from the MAP Fund. *Sucktion* has been produced internationally. *Crescent City* premiered in Los Angeles in 2012. He has been commissioned to write or teach ekphrastic poetry for the Weisman Museum (Minneapolis), Studio Museum in Harlem, MOCA, SFMOMA, the Getty, and the Hammer.

Of "In the End, They Were Born on TV," Kearney writes: "About six months into my wife N's very difficult pregnancy, her OB/GYN called to tell me she had transferred N to a new doctor. It turns out the new doctor was a star of a reality TV show about difficult pregnancies and how such challenging work affects the doctors' own families and relationships. It wasn't long before the show's producer asked N whether she would be willing to appear on the show.

"Through most of her pregnancy, N had hyperemesis—morning sickness on steroids. She would vomit dozens of times a day; even water made her vomit. She was on an IV for nutrition and was at home on bed rest, and, as it happened, she became familiar with the TV show during those months she spent lying very still on the couch. She found it helpful to watch other women in similar circumstances, so she agreed to be on the show.

"The poem pivots on a shoot the crew did at our home when, in pursuit of emotional exposition, the interviewer pressed us to discuss the miscarriage that had terminated N's last pregnancy. Each time we tried to tell the story, some external sound—dogs and low-flying aircraft—ruined the take. The details with which we told the story diminished with each interrupted retelling. As the poem says: 'It was horrible.'

"Still, the crew was professional and kind. The doctors gave my wife the best care we could have imagined. To my knowledge, the show—we were a two-episode arc!—never aired. We have it on DVD, though. We'll show it to the twins when they're a bit older."

JENNIFER KEITH is a web content writer for Johns Hopkins Medicine. She attended the University of Virginia and graduated from the American University in Washington, DC, with a degree in cinema. She received the 2014 John Elsberg poetry prize. She lives in Baltimore, Maryland, where she collects tea and plays bass guitar for the rock band Batworth Stone.

Of "Eating Walnuts," Keith writes: "As a child, I read about a squirrel learning to eat hazelnuts through trial and error. I was impressed that this instinct-driven animal had to teach itself, making several unsuccessful attempts before finding the most effective method.

"My late father was a painter with unusual spatial intelligence and perhaps a touch of OCD. He loved showing my mother and me better, more efficient ways of doing small things like loading the dishwasher. This wasn't nearly as exasperating as it sounds.

"My current job involves spending time with neurosurgeons who are fantastically creative in discovering new ways to access brain lesions while avoiding damage to surrounding tissue and structures. Thus the poem takes on another layer of meaning for me."

DAVID KIRBY was born in Baton Rouge, Louisiana, in 1944, and teaches at Florida State University. He is the author most recently of *The Biscuit*

Joint (Louisiana State University Press, 2013) and *A Wilderness of Monkeys* (Hanging Loose Press, 2014). For more, see www.davidkirby.com.

Of "Is Spot in Heaven?" Kirby writes: "At the heart of this poem is Sam Cooke's haunting ballad 'A Change Is Gonna Come,' in which a man worn down by life on earth says he doesn't want to leave because he doesn't know what's on the other side. That's a question that vexes both theologians and children alike, one that I answer the way one can only in a poem, where the poet has the opportunity to invent a world that contains everything this world doesn't. When I look back at my poems, it seems that most of them are little problem-solving machines; this one is no different.

"Currently I'm reading Andrew Grant Jackson's *1965: The Most Revolutionary Year in Music*, a book about a time when, in his words, 'You couldn't turn on the radio without hearing a new classic,' including Cooke's song but also 'Like a Rolling Stone,' 'Papa's Got a Brand New Bag,' 'Respect,' 'The Sound of Silence,' 'Yesterday,' 'People Get Ready,' and hundreds of others. How'd that happen? A statistician I know said it's pretty simple: events tend to occur at more or less regular intervals, though sometimes they occur more often in a given time period and sometimes less so.

"That said, individual persistence has to count for something. Of the recording sessions that led to the release of the Stones' '(I Can't Get No) Satisfaction,' the band knocked out the greatest rock song ever without even trying because, as Jackson says, they were always trying. 'Is Spot in Heaven?' marks my sixth appearance in the *Best American Poetry* series, yet my first poem didn't appear there till I was fifty-four years old. So hang in there, you poets."

ANDREW KOZMA was born in Tucson, Arizona, in 1976. He lives in Houston, Texas, where he teaches technical writing at the University of Houston. His book of poems, *City of Regret* (Zone 3 Press, 2007), won the Zone 3 First Book Award.

Of "Ode to the Common Housefly," Kozma writes: "I guess there are two things at work here: the form and the subject. The subject is easy. I've always been fascinated by insects, and a few years ago I decided to write a series of odes in celebration of those insects that most people (except entomologists, I suppose) would not celebrate. The form is my attempting to mix earnestness with pomposity, the ornate with the mundane, trying to pack so much into the poem (sonically and linguistically) that it bleeds outside its own lines, finally transforming into the honest appreciation of a housefly couched in a psalm-like prayer."

HAILEY LEITHAUSER was born in Baltimore, Maryland, in 1954 and grew up in Florida and Maryland. She is the author of *Swoop* (Graywolf, 2013). Her work appears in *Copper Nickel*, *The Gettysburg Review*, *Poetry*, *The Yale Review*, and *The Best American Poetry 2010* and *2014*. She has lived up and down the East Coast and has had too many jobs to count, her last full-time gig as the senior reference librarian at the Department of Energy. She now teaches occasionally at The Writer's Center in Bethesda, Maryland.

Of "The Pickpocket Song," Leithauser writes: " 'Pickpocket' came to be when I was muttering around one day last winter, whining online about a terminal lack of inspiration, and possibly to shut me up, Amy Beeder devised an exercise for us to try in which she sent me a line from a draft she was toying with to use anywhere within a poem of my own. I was then to send her a line from my draft for her to incorporate, so that each poem would end up sharing the two lines.

"Neither of us knew what the other person's title or subject matter was beforehand so there was much joy and long-distance clinking of glasses when the lines actually ended up playing quite well off one another and we both got a nice poem out of the deal. (If you want to find out which were the borrowed lines, you can read both poems in the 2014 summer issue of *32 Poems*. As to who wrote which line, I'll never tell.) We liked the exercise so much that now we're talking about putting together an anthology as soon as we can come up with a dozen or so like-minded writers to pair off and a snappy title."

DANA LEVIN was born in Los Angeles, California, in 1965 and grew up in the Mojave Desert. She is the author of three books of poetry: *In the Surgical Theatre* (Copper Canyon Press, 1999), *Wedding Day* (Copper Canyon Press, 2005), and *Sky Burial* (Copper Canyon Press, 2011). A recipient of awards from the Rona Jaffe, Whiting, and Guggenheim foundations, Levin splits her time between Santa Fe, New Mexico, and Maryville University in St. Louis, where she serves as Distinguished Writer in Residence. This is her first appearance in *The Best American Poetry*.

Of "Watching the Sea Go," Levin writes: "I was staying on a beloved part of the Northern California coast intending to write, but all I kept doing was taking thirty-second videos of the sea. It seemed like such an absurd activity (the sea was right there!), but I was compelled. On the page I'd been troubling our environmental future; perhaps the videos were little stays against the End."

PATRICIA LOCKWOOD was born in Fort Wayne, Indiana, in 1982, and raised in all the worst cities of the Midwest. She is the author of the poetry collections *Motherland Fatherland Homelandsexuals* (Penguin Books, 2014) and *Balloon Pop Outlaw Black* (Octopus Books, 2012).

Of "See a Furious Waterfall Without Water," Lockwood writes: "In 1969, they drained Niagara Falls. In 2010, I was messing around on my computer, and I saw a headline enjoining me to look at 'a waterfall without water.' I clicked through and found a photoset of empty Niagara. It had not occurred to me that a waterfall could be conditional, like a lap. The character, all of a sudden, stood there quite solidly, fixing his cuffs and looking generally dissipated, needing nothing so much as a drink. It was apparent he had a wedding to go to."

DORA MALECH was born in New Haven, Connecticut, in 1981 and grew up in Maryland. She earned degrees at Yale University and the University of Iowa Writers' Workshop. She has received a Frederick M. Clapp Poetry Writing Fellowship from Yale, a Truman Capote Fellowship and a Teaching-Writing Fellowship from the Iowa Writers' Workshop, a Glenn Schaeffer Poetry Award, a Writer's Fellowship at the Civitella Ranieri Center in Italy, and a Ruth Lilly Poetry Fellowship from the Poetry Foundation. The Waywiser Press published her first full-length collection of poems, *Shore Ordered Ocean*, in 2009, and the Cleveland State University Poetry Center published her second collection, *Say So*, in 2011. Her poetry has been adapted into short films for the Motionpoems series, and it has been featured in a musical collaboration with composer Jacob Cooper in his song cycle *Silver Threads* (Nonesuch Records, 2014). Malech lives in Baltimore, Maryland, where she joined the faculty of the Writing Seminars at Johns Hopkins University as an assistant professor of poetry in 2014.

Of "Party Games," Malech writes: "After piñatas made appearances at a friend's baby shower a few years ago and another friend's bachelorette party this past year, my childhood fascination was revived. Watching some of the kindest, gentlest women I knew beating a papier-mâché animal with a stick got me thinking about the complicated role of play, especially violent play, in childhood and adulthood. Not all of this thinking made its way into the poem, and there are numerous cultural and religious traditions and a rich global history of the piñata that didn't make their way explicitly into the scene. I focused in on specific visual memories: the moment when the stick we were using to hit the piñata (actually just an ancient wooden-handled ice-scraper from my car) broke under the force of the blows, the smile beneath the blindfold, the two-fisted grip, and so forth. In revising the poem, I chose to specify the pronouns 'she' and 'we,' but never to specify the age of the participants, so the poem could be read as a child's game, as I had witnessed and experienced many times. It felt important to me on a personal level that the poem functioned as a palimpsest, with adult violence enacted in a child's game and a child's sense of play revived in adulthood."

DONNA MASINI was born in Brooklyn in 1954 and has lived in New York ever since. She is the author of two collections of poems—*Turning to Fiction* (W. W. Norton, 2004) and *That Kind of Danger* (Beacon Press, 1994), which was selected by Mona Van Duyn for the Barnard Women Poet's Prize—and a novel, *About Yvonne* (Norton, 1998). She is an associate professor of English at Hunter College, where she teaches in the MFA creative writing program. She has recently finished *The Good Enough Mother*, a novel.

Of "Anxieties," Masini writes: "After finishing a novel, I was in that drifting place, scribbling, slowly collecting drafts toward a new book I'm calling *4:30 Movie*. Terrance Hayes gave me the idea of the 'word scramble poem'—a form he'd 'invented.' As with any prompt, it might or might not lead somewhere, but there's always a surprise (once you find 'orgasm' imbedded in 'smorgasbord' it starts you off somewhere unexpected) and my first attempt ended up as a couple of lines in another poem: 'If you think in anagrams, / parades and drapes, diapers, rape, despair and aspire / all come out of paradise.' In these poems I'll give myself different formal conditions, but every line must end (and in some poems begin) with one of the words that comes out of the scramble. Sometimes I use it to 'warm up.' Here's the thing: I've always loved watching words nesting or recombining inside other words. As a kid I'd look at a street sign or Corn Flakes box and see how many words I could find inside a word or phrase. I think it calmed me down. So this process feels deeply familiar. Sometimes I try it when I'm anxious about writing—a sort of 'meditation meets Boggle'—hence the title of this poem."

Born in Trenton, New Jersey, in 1972, AIREA D. MATTHEWS is a Cave Canem and Callaloo Fellow. She is a lecturer of English at the University of Michigan, Ann Arbor, where she earned her MFA. She is the co–executive editor of *The Offing*.

Matthews writes: " 'If My Late Grandmother Were Gertrude Stein' started as a Facebook status shortly after I read Stein's *Tender Buttons*. I began to consider the ways in which my grandmother, a fifth-grade dropout during the Great Depression, grasped at language to share her fractured narratives. She didn't have any direct experience with modernism as a formal construct. However, I noticed a relationship between Gertrude Stein and my grandmother's disparate lives and identities. The poem serves as a seemingly impossible bridge between the three of us."

JAMAAL MAY writes and records poetry, music, and short films. He is the author of *Hum* and founder of Organic Weapon Arts, which he codirects with his partner, Tarfia Faizullah.

Of "There Are Birds Here," May writes: "I wanted to throw my half cent into the national conversation about Detroit. A deluge of thoughtless speaking on the subject drove me to reach for craft elements that would help me argue for attention to the space between shadow and light—the space we all actually exist in. The bird figuration came in when I jokingly said, 'Hey, there are birds in there, too,' after I noticed that reviewers latched on to the metal in *Hum* but usually overlooked the feathers. They also show up because I'm obsessed with the hypothesis that context is more important than object. Birds were among the pet objects I heard writers express their ire for seeing in 'too many poems' (too many for what, I wonder). The layer beneath is 'I'm tired of birds appearing in the same context.' But since we don't invent a new language for every book anyway, are we ever really doing much more than looking for a new context when we decide to put this word next to that one? So if I can make a plain, old bird do real work in a poem, I get to start the conversation about limited thinking right there. I cribbed the negation move from Alan Dugan's 'Closing Time at the Second Avenue Deli.' He never lets the metaphor rest, even though he knows it can't be taken back after we've seen it. It's a great way to show complexity rather than beg others to acknowledge it. My closing lines got worked and reworked until the music and sense synced with the enjambments. It creates a tension between sentence and line that puts ambivalence in the reader's body, which can't be achieved by simply saying 'this is complicated.' Michael Bazzett, an excellent poet and high school teacher, told me he and his students call this a 'pump fake,' a basketball move in which you quickly pretend to shoot so that the defender flinches or jumps to block you, making it easy to just go around them.

"At the time of the first draft, the bankruptcy was a lead story. If it wasn't the media talking about my city like no one lived here (we do) and no one thrives here (I do), then it was the lazy art. Everyone in Brooklyn thought they were the first to photograph decay porn. Our own glowing send-ups to Motown and one-sided rants about how awesome we are, while encouraging, began to feel as thoughtless as the doom-saying. I wanted to share something about the complexity of this place in a way that a young student could understand, in a way that any reader could memorize, and still have layers for the advanced lit-heads to peel back. None of these pleasures are either pretentious or trivial. Since publication, 'There Are Birds Here' has been republished by the *New York Times* Learning Network and translated into other languages. It receives thousands of reads a day online, and an ACLU chapter vice president recently used the poem to explain why a housing class action lawsuit was important. The poem has left me encouraged in this belief: When I flatly state my opinion, all you can do is agree or fight me. When I artfully present my interior, you have to take the third option, the one you've always had: think."

LAURA MCCULLOUGH was born in 1960. Her most recent books include *Rigger Death & Hoist Another* (poems, Black Lawrence Press, 2013), *Ripple & Snap* (prose poem hybrid, ELP Press, 2014), *Shutters: Voices: Wind* (dramatic monologues, ELP Press, 2014), and *The Smashing House* (short fiction, ELP Press, 2014). She has edited two anthologies, *The Room and the World: Essays on the Poet Stephen Dunn* (University of Syracuse Press, 2014) and *A Sense of Regard: essays on poetry and race* (University of Georgia Press, 2015). She teaches at Brookdale Community College in New Jersey and is on the faculty of the Sierra Nevada low-residency MFA. She is the founding editor of *Mead: The Magazine of Literature and Libations*.

McCullough writes: "'There Were Only Dandelions' is placed almost in the center of the book that became *Rigger Death & Hoist Another* (Black Lawrence Press), named from the title of a more narrative poem, the second in the collection. A dandelion was the initiating image that sent me on the series of self-queries that manifested this collection, and my ongoing concern, sorrow, and wonder about the world of masculinities and of masculine violence, and, increasingly, violence in general and globally. The cover of the book is a dandelion head in contrast, not white against black, but a black head against white. I was writing in response to my previous book of poems, *Panic* (Alice James Books), which were all third-person narratives located on the Jersey Shore, not a single first-person I in any of them. That book is deeply emotionally autobiographical, but the character of self does not show up in them; it was all about witness and narrative distance.

"'There Were Only Dandelions' is something of a manifesto, an assertion against distance, an effort to be both complicit in my own work and more genuine, to find the confluence between mind and storification, the sensual and the cerebral, the fictive and the poetic. I am searching in my work for ways to collude many opposites, or things that are seeming oppositional, to colocate the miniature and the massive, to find the juxtaposition in what may present as incongruous. And I wanted to begin to shed veils, the things that occlude our understanding of self as well as obscure our apprehension by others; in a word, I wanted to be more genuine. Yet maybe that is why I landed this poem in the center of the book rather than forefronting it. It scared me some. Maybe that's where we have to go, though, toward what we fear?"

Rajiv Mohabir was born in London in 1981 and has lived in Orlando, New York, Honolulu, Jaipur, and Varanasi. Winner of the 2014 Intro Prize in Poetry by Four Way Books for his first full-length collection, *The Taxidermist's Cut* (spring 2016), he received fellowships from Voices of Our Nation's Artist foundation, Kundiman, and the American Institute of Indian Studies language program. He received his MFA in Poetry and Translation from Queens College, CUNY, where he was editor in chief of the *Ozone Park* literary journal. He is pursuing a PhD in English from the University of Hawai'i.

Of "Dove," Mohabir writes: "I call this a 'chutney poem' because it mimics 'chutney music,' a genre of Indo-Caribbean folksong developed by Sundar Popo. It has a Guyanese Hindi chorus that informs the following couplets and draws from my three languages: Guyanese Hindi/Bhojpuri, Creole, and English. To this music/poetic themes of loss, love, and separation are vital.

"I find myself attempting to harness the palimpsest of Caribbean poetic sense and channeling it into a queer sonnet. I imagine the *dholak*, harmonium, and my Aji singing from India to Guyana to Toronto to New York to Orlando. I purposely queer the sonnet as a slyly civil anti-colonial measure to make it as queer as an Indian in South America; a sari in sea-trunk.

"To create a form I connect to my family's own folk literature. Every poem in this genre I've written is singable to the tune of 'Kaise Bani.' To engage with the American poetic landscape it must be honest: something syncretic, something musical."

AIMEE NEZHUKUMATATHIL was born in Chicago, Illinois, in 1974. She received undergraduate and graduate degrees from Ohio State University. She is the author of *Miracle Fruit* (2003), winner of the ForeWord Poetry Book of the Year Award; *At the Drive-In Volcano* (2007), winner of the Balcones Prize; and *Lucky Fish* (2011), winner of the gold medal in poetry from the Independent Publishers Book Awards, all from Tupelo Press. With Ross Gay, she is coauthor of the epistolary chapbook *Lace & Pyrite: Letters from Two Gardens* (Organic Weapon Arts, 2014). She is a professor of English and a recipient of a Chancellor's Medal at the State University of New York at Fredonia.

Of "Upon Hearing the News You Buried Our Dog," Nezhukumatathil writes: "One of my favorite stars to scorch up the summer sky is Albireo, the head of the swan, in the constellation Cygnus. In the second century, Ptolemy included Cygnus in his famous list of forty-eight constellations. When I was eight months pregnant with my youngest child, I received a note from a former love that the dog we once raised together in grad school was days away from dying of old age. Of course I was devastated about the loss, and yet—the bright kicks of my baby boy pulled me toward a new life, a new sky. In thinking about finding solace in nature, I'm reminded of the marginalia found in Ptolemy's sky notebooks: 'I know I am mortal by nature . . . but when I trace at my pleasure the windings to and fro of the heavenly bodies, I no longer touch earth with my feet.'"

D. NURKSE was born in New York City in 1949. He is the author of ten collections of poetry, most recently *A Night in Brooklyn*, *The Border Kingdom*, *Burnt Island*, and *The Fall* (Alfred A. Knopf, 2012, 2008, 2005, and 2002). He has also taught at the Rikers Island Correctional Facility and written for human rights organizations. A recipient of poetry awards from the American Academy of Arts and Letters, the Guggenheim Foundation, the Whiting Foundation, the National Endowment for the Arts, the Tanne Foundation, and the New York Foundation for the Arts, he lives in Brooklyn and teaches at Sarah Lawrence College.

Nurkse writes: "'Plutonium' visits the threshold of the nuclear age. I'm moved by Richard Rhodes's excellent book *The Making of the Atom*

Bomb. My poem re-creates a few scenes and incorporates part of a quote from Neils Bohr. The image of the man with his eyeball in his hand recurs in accounts of Hiroshima. It feels like a metaphor for shock you can't assimilate. But it isn't a symbol. It happened. That maddening sense of a dream becoming real is at the core of the era. Suddenly, squiggles on a chalkboard could kill not just people but civilizations. I'm a child of that moment. But I haven't digested it, though its challenges are still in front of my nose. How deep these nightmares are buried in my generation's psyche is marked by the speed with which we emigrated to the Internet, a world without death."

TANYA OLSON was born in Springfield, Illinois, in 1967. She currently lives in Silver Spring, Maryland, and teaches English at UMBC (University of Maryland, Baltimore County). Her first book, *Boyishly*, was published by YesYes Books in 2013 and received a 2014 American Book Award. In 2010, she won a Discovery/*Boston Review* prize, and she was named a 2011 Lambda Fellow by the Lambda Literary Foundation.

Olson writes: " '54 Prince' began as a high five to scientists for coming up with such an awesome term as "Goldilocks planet." I thought the phrase gave us narrative-craving humans an immediate idea of what the planets were like but still kept them mysterious; just like a fairy tale, the term taught us something important and made the planets seem just this side of impossible. Why fifty-four of them? I always think about reading a poem aloud and the number repeats a lot, so I needed something that sounded musical and falling. Fifty-four it was, even though Kepler has currently spotted only about a dozen planets that orbit a star at the right distance to allow for liquid water. (That's what a Goldilocks planet technically is.) Why Prince? I wondered what else all these 'good enough' planets would need to survive. Wouldn't life be easier if each planet had its own Prince—brilliant, a little off, possibly extraterrestrial anyway? 'Worried Man Blues' is a brilliant, eerie song, especially in Carter Family renditions. Mother Maybelle and Prince fit nicely together at the end and lend the poem an air of being a little, American fairy tale."

RON PADGETT grew up in Tulsa and has lived mostly in New York City since 1960. He has won a Guggenheim Fellowship, the American Academy of Arts and Letters poetry award, the Shelley Memorial Award, and grants from the National Endowment for the Arts. His *How Long* was a Pulitzer Prize finalist in poetry and his *Collected Poems* won the *Los Angeles Times* Prize for the best poetry book of 2014 and the William

Carlos Williams Award from the Poetry Society of America. "Survivor Guilt" forms part of his new collection, *Alone and Not Alone* (Coffee House Press). Padgett has translated works by Guillaume Apollinaire, Pierre Reverdy, and Blaise Cendrars. His own work has been translated into eighteen languages.

ALAN MICHAEL PARKER was born in New York in 1961. He is the author of eight collections of poetry, including *The Ladder* (Tupelo Press, 2016), and three novels, and is the coeditor of various works about poetry, including *The Manifesto Project* (University of Akron Press, 2016). He is Douglas C. Houchens Professor of English at Davidson College, and also teaches in the University of Tampa low-residency MFA program.

Of "Candying Mint," Parker writes: "I have been asking questions in my poems for years—of Simone de Beauvoir, Odysseas Elytis, Du Fu, Ludwig Wittgenstein, *et alia*—as I have come across their wisdom in my meanderings. Here, reading and asking questions of Martin Buber's ideas inspired the poem.

"I like to cook, and I often find meaning in my kitchen. In this case, I candied mint as part of the finale to a holiday blowout with family and friends. The recipe and the occasion were special, and stuck with me for nine months, when the first draft of the poem was written. The final draft of the poem begins with instructions that can be followed precisely; it's an easy dish to make, part herb and part metaphysical inquiry."

CATHERINE PIERCE was born in Wilmington, Delaware, in 1978. She is the author of *The Girls of Peculiar* (Saturnalia, 2012) and *Famous Last Words* (2008, winner of the Saturnalia Books Poetry Prize). Her third book, *The Tornado Is the World*, is forthcoming from Saturnalia in 2016. She is an associate professor at Mississippi State University, where she codirects the creative writing program.

Of "Relevant Details," Pierce writes: "This poem came out of a failure of memory. I wanted to write about a bar I'd gone to once, many years and many cities ago, and I could not for the life of me remember what it was called, which seemed an inauspicious beginning. I started writing anyway, trusting—or at least hoping—that if I kept going, the poem would eventually reveal its significance. For a long time, it didn't. I was just riffing on this idea of imprecise memory, and the whole thing was starting to feel gimmicky. I almost gave up, but instead decided to see what happened when I stepped back and acknowledged the gimmick directly. Once I gave myself permission to do that—to revise toward the problem rather than away from it—the poem broke open for me and I was able to push it until I could see what it was really about."

DONALD PLATT was born in Coral Gables, Florida, in 1957. He is a professor of English and teaches in the MFA program at Purdue University. His poems have been included twice before in *The Best American Poetry* series (the 2000 and 2006 editions). His fifth book of poems, *Tornadoesque*, is forthcoming from CavanKerry Press's Notable Voices Series in 2016. His other volumes of poetry are *Dirt Angels* (New Issues Press, 2009), *My Father Says Grace* (University of Arkansas Press, 2007), *Cloud Atlas* (Purdue University Press, 2002), and *Fresh Peaches, Fireworks, & Guns* (Purdue University Press, 1994). In 1996 and again in 2011, he won fellowships from the National Endowment for the Arts.

Platt writes: "I remember the genesis of 'The Main Event' very clearly. The day after my fifty-sixth birthday, I read the front-page obituary of boxer Emile Griffith in *The New York Times* (July 23, 2013) by Richard Goldstein. The article recounted the shocking story of the third Griffith vs. Paret fight. Having never encountered this story before, I couldn't get it out of my head. Eager for more particulars, I turned to the Internet and pulled up all the source material I could find about Griffith, Paret, and their fatal boxing match. I went on to watch the entire TV footage of the March 24, 1962, fight with Ruby Goldstein as referee and Don Dunphy as the ABC announcer. At the end of that footage, after Benny 'Kid' Paret had been carried out of the ring on a stretcher, they replayed the minute and a half leading up to the knockout in slow motion. It seemed much slower than the slow-mo of today's televised boxing matches.

"The replay lasted three minutes and seven seconds and included some of the most brutal boxing I had ever witnessed. Even on this first viewing, I noted the detached tone with which some of the commentators described the precise mayhem that Griffith inflicted on Paret, who wouldn't go down because he was caught in the ropes. The unintentionally ironic resonances of Dunphy's final words on the broadcast, in which he lists the 'hosts' of the event, were also singularly striking. Next, I watched on YouTube the 2005 *Ring of Fire*, a documentary about Emile Griffith, directed by Dan Klores and Ron Berger. It provided the context for the fight and would later be the source of most of the quotes I used in the poem.

"From the moment I saw Griffith's obituary, I knew that I wanted to write about the fight, the sexually charged insults at the weigh-in, and how the fight's aftermath affected Emile, Paret's family, the boxing 'industry,' and, therefore, the whole nation. The undercurrents of that old story from 1962 are with us today. Nearly three months before Griffith died, NBA player Jason Collins came out and would become the first openly gay active player in any of the four major professional sports in the United States. As of this writing, no active player in the NFL has publicly acknowledged that he is gay. Emile Griffith showed a similar reluctance to talk openly about his sexual orientation. Reflecting years later on the verbal abuse that he received from Paret at the weigh-in on March 24, 1962, Emile declared angrily, 'I wasn't nobody's faggot.'"

CLAUDIA RANKINE was born in 1963. She is the author of five collections of poetry, including *Citizen* and *Don't Let Me Be Lonely*, and the plays *Provenance of Beauty: A South Bronx Travelogue*, commissioned by the Foundry Theatre, and *Existing Conditions* (written collaboratively with Casey Llewellyn). Rankine is coeditor of the *American Women Poets in the Twenty-First Century* series with Wesleyan University Press and *The Racial Imaginary: Writers on Race in the Life of the Mind* with Fence Books. A recipient of awards and fellowships from the Academy of American Poets, the American Academy of Arts and Letters, the Lannan Foundation, the NAACP, Poets & Writers, and the National Endowment for the Arts, she teaches at Pomona College and is a chancellor of the Academy of American Poets.

Of this excerpt from *Citizen*, Rankine writes: "Jim Crow Road was photographed by Michael David Murphy. When I first saw the image I was sure it was Photoshopped. I was wrong. The road is located in Flowery Branch, Georgia. Sometimes when I am waiting for something else to happen I wonder what's it's like to have a signifier of our racial caste system as a destination, a home address."

RAPHAEL RUBINSTEIN was born in Lawrence, Kansas, in 1955. After graduating from Bennington College, he moved to New York City in 1979, where, apart from several years in Milan, Italy, he has lived ever since. His poetry publications include *The Basement of the Café Rilke* (Hard Press, 1997), *The Afterglow of Minor Pop Masterpieces* (Make Now, 2005), *The Cry of Unbalance* (Song Cave, 2013), and the forthcoming *A Geniza* (Granary Books). He is also the author of *Postcards from Alphaville* (Hard Press, 2000), *Polychrome Profusion: Selected Art Criticism 1990–2002* (Hard Press, 2003), and *The Miraculous* (Paper Monument, 2014). He has received the award of Chevalier in the Order of Arts and Letters from the French government and a Warhol Foundation/Creative Capital arts writers grant. From 1994 to 2007 he was an editor at *Art in America*. He is currently professor of critical studies at the University of Houston School of Art.

Rubinstein writes: "As a commuting teacher, and a longtime fan of the poetry of voyage epitomized by Valery Larbaud and Blaise Cendrars, I often start poems in transit. 'Poem Begun on a Train' was written in the fall of 2013 in response to an invitation from Andrew Ridker to contribute to *Privacy Policy: The Anthology of Surveillance Poetics* (Black Ocean). Gradually, what began as a poem about its own making led me, via increasingly dark scenarios of readership, from tautology to history. The Scottish modernist poet Hugh MacDiarmid, who was appropriating texts many decades before the advent of 'conceptual writing,' supplied not only an instance of a poet under state surveillance but also a model for the recasting of found prose as verse, something I do throughout the poem. Another person on my mind, though unnamed, was Franco Moretti, an innovative literary scholar known for his concept of 'distant reading.' The 2013–2014 Whitney Museum exhibition mentioned at the end of the poem focused on mostly forgotten 1970s New York performance art, including Squat Theatre, a group of Hungarian exiles whose theater was a storefront space on West 23rd Street. Soon after arriving in New York I saw their wild multimedia piece *Andy Warhol's Last Love*, which included a recital of Kafka's 'An Imperial Message.' Distressingly, Kafka has turned out to be as relevant to the twenty-first century as he was to the twentieth."

NATALIE SCENTERS-ZAPICO, born in 1988, is from the sister cities of El Paso, Texas, and Cd. Juárez, Chihuahua. She is the author of *The Verging Cities* (Center for Literary Publishing, 2015). She teaches creative writing and English at Juan Diego Catholic High School and splits her time between El Paso–Cd. Juárez, Oviedo, and Salt Lake City. Learn more at nataliescenterszapico.com.

Of "Endnotes on Ciudad Juárez," Scenters-Zapico writes: "As an adolescent, I loved reading history books and became very familiar with Chicago/Turabian style. As a game, I would read these histories by beginning with the endnotes and find each corresponding reference in the main passage. I was fascinated by the way the focus of the book changed simply by giving the limelight to the endnotes. This poem is an exploration of how the order of a book, especially one that claims to be historical or academic, holds two stories. One, which contains the main subject of the text; the other, the hidden back material that often presents secondary stories thought not worthy of mention in the main text by the author. In 'Endnotes on Ciudad Juárez' I wanted to give Cd. Juárez the place of front material without neglecting the fact that it is often placed as back material in U.S. history. In this way, I hope to give the reader an opportunity to put into practice the way that I read history books as an adolescent, thereby recognizing the day-to-day ways in which Cd. Juárez is important to U.S. consciousness."

EVIE SHOCKLEY was born in Nashville, Tennessee, in 1965 and reborn in Durham, North Carolina, in 1996. Her poetry publications include *the new black* (Wesleyan, 2011), winner of the 2012 Hurston/Wright Legacy Award in Poetry; *a half-red sea* (Carolina Wren Press, 2006); and two chapbooks. She is also the author of *Renegade Poetics: Black Aesthetics and Formal Innovation in African American Poetry* (Iowa, 2011). She is a creative writing editor for *Feminist Studies* and an associate professor of English at Rutgers University–New Brunswick. She has made her home in Jersey City, New Jersey, now for more consecutive years than in any place she has lived in since Nashville, a fact that she finds shocking.

Of "legend," Shockley writes: "I have always loved form, forms, in poetry: given forms, like the sonnet and the ghazal; visual form, as in concrete poetry or other approaches that purposefully use the space of the page; and procedural forms, such as the constraints the Oulipians have developed. This poem falls largely within that last category. The constraint it employs is called *univocalism*, which means that only one of the vowels is used throughout the poem. In this case, it's the vowel 'e,' to the exclusion of all the others. Univocalism is challenging, but fun to write, and it can create powerful sonic effects.

"As I recall, I wrote this poem at the very beginning of a six-week period I spent in Asheville, North Carolina, during the summer of 2012. I'd hoped this would be a window in which I would write a lot, but that turned out to have been extremely optimistic. I was there to teach two courses for the Bread Loaf School of English, and any time that wasn't devoted to work I spent enjoying Asheville and seeing my friends in the area. But in my first days in town, I sat down with my notebook and used the formal constraint to jump-start a poem out of thin air. The story of Fern and Bess, two 'clever femmes' who were working against constraints of their own, seemed to write itself, as I searched for words that fit the bill. I decided to teach the form in my creative writing course a few weeks later. My students came up with some strong, energetic, vibrant poems, thanks in part to a constraint that won't allow you to slide by on your go-to words and phrases or rely on mindless patterns of syntax."

CHARLES SIMIC is a poet, essayist, and translator. He is the recipient of many awards, including the Pulitzer Prize, the Griffin Prize, and a MacArthur Fellowship. In 2007 Simic was appointed the fifteenth United States Poet Laureate. *The Lunatic*, his new volume of poetry, and *The Life of Images*, a book of his selected prose, were published in the spring of 2015. He was the guest editor of *The Best American Poetry 1992*.

Of "So Early in the Morning," Simic writes: "My friends have been dying over the last few years, so that's behind this poem of mine."

SANDRA SIMONDS was born in Washington, DC, in 1977 and now lives in Tallahassee, Florida. She is professor of English and humanities at Thomas University in Thomasville, Georgia, and is the author of four collections of poetry: *Ventura Highway in the Sunshine* (Saturnalia Books, 2015), *The Sonnets* (Bloof Books, 2014), *Mother Was a Tragic Girl* (Cleveland State University Press, 2012), and *Warsaw Bikini* (Bloof Books, 2009).

Of "Similitude at Versailles," Simonds writes: "This poem, from my fourth book, *Ventura Highway in the Sunshine*, is part of a series of poems that deals with how we teach humanities courses at the university. Before I started my job as a professor, I had always taught literature, not humanities, and I was interested in exploring and interrogating the humanities textbook and canon formation as a poetry project—what do we leave out of the humanities, what is included in the humanities? What voices are forever lost? What voices stick around and echo into the future? I came to the conclusion, as so many have before me, that it's the minor voices that get left out (like mine?), and I tried to think about my own life as a poet. What are the material circumstances of my life and how do these material circumstances affect my work as a poet? What does it mean to try to write a poem in a house when children need to be fed, when cartoons are distracting you from trying to write, when you are living paycheck to paycheck? I wanted to include the material circumstances of my life to be, not the background of my poem, but rather the foreground to make a point about the humanities. What does it mean to be a working mother in the twenty-first century? Will my voice also be lost? Saved?"

ED SKOOG was born in Topeka, Kansas, in 1971. He has lived in New Orleans, Southern California, and Montana, and currently lives in Seattle. He has published two books of poems, *Mister Skylight* (Copper Canyon Press, 2009) and *Rough Day* (Copper Canyon, 2013), which won the Washington State Book Award in poetry. In addition to sometimes teaching at Seattle's Hugo House, he is codirector of Writing Week at the Idyllwild Arts Summer Program, is cohost (with the novelist J. Robert Lennon) of the podcast *Lunch Box, with Ed and John*, and is poetry editor of *Okey-Panky*.

Of "The Macarena," Skoog writes: "I think I took a long time paying my dues, a process that started only after school began to wear off. This poem recalls a few months of that time. Twenty-three years old that summer, I'd rented an apartment in the Sunflower Hotel in Abilene and tried to write a novel about the people who worked at the Eisenhower Presidential Library, which resembles a college campus. A fountain burbles in the chapel where he's interred. Long hours there. In my family, Eisenhower is remembered as kindly and local. I didn't have enough dissonance, perhaps, to sustain such a narrative. It was a severe, lonely time. Coffee talked to me from the stovetop percolator. I almost got arrested for climbing a grain silo to watch the sunrise. I was naïve about writing and love. Still am, I hope. When small-town loneliness got to me, I'd drive to Kansas City and visit a friend who was living by the art museum. She was gearing up to move to New York and maybe I'd come, too. Instead I abandoned the novel, and novel writing, and moved to Seattle for another love. Eighteen years later I wrote this poem."

A. E. STALLINGS was born in 1968. She studied classics in Athens, Georgia, and since 1999 has lived in Athens, Greece. She has published three collections of poems, *Archaic Smile* (University of Evansville Press, 1999), *Hapax* (Northwestern University Press, 2006), and *Olives* (Northwestern University Press, 2012). Her verse translation of Lucretius, *The Nature of Things*, was published by Penguin Classics in 2007 and her verse translation of Hesiod's *Works and Days* is forthcoming from the same publisher. She has received fellowships from the Guggenheim, United States Artists, and MacArthur foundations, as well as a translation grant from the National Endowment for the Arts.

Of "Ajar," Stallings writes: "I've spent the last couple of years at work on a verse translation of Hesiod's eighth-century BC almanac, *Works and Days*, for Penguin Classics. Hesiod's is the first version we have of the story of Pandora and the Jar. (It's better known as Pandora's Box;

but in Hesiod's time, the storage vessels were jars.) So it was natural to conflate that with home life. (The offending washing machine has since been replaced, thank the gods.) In Greek, the word usually translated as 'hope' ('elpis') is more ambiguous, and could even mean 'anxiety' about the future. I think that was in the back of my mind, too. The last line, it strikes me in retrospect, is a pretty Hesiodic sentiment. The formal structure, with the two strands of rhymes running through the tercets, showed up from the get-go, but it didn't occur to me to do the (perhaps obvious) thing of cracking open the lines until relatively late in revision. The space, or pause, gave it a bit more breathing room on the page. The punning title probably came at about the same moment."

SUSAN TERRIS was born in St. Louis, Missouri, in 1937 and lives in San Francisco. Her most recent book is *Ghost of Yesterday: New & Selected Poems* (Marsh Hawk Press, 2013). She is the author of six books of poetry, fifteen chapbooks, and three artist's books. She had a prior career in the field of children's books. Farrar, Straus and Giroux was the primary publisher for her twenty-one children's and young adult books. She is the editor of *Spillway Magazine*. Her book *Memos* will be published by Omnidawn in 2015. See www.susanterris.com.

Of "Memo to the Former Child Prodigy," Terris writes: "As a child, I desperately wanted to be a prodigy, though at that time I would have used the word 'star.' I was a dancer, a competitive swimmer, a wanna-be actress, a curious student, and I had already had a story published in a national teenage magazine. My parents rejected the prodigy notion, telling me calmly, 'Too public. We don't do things that way.' And if I asked them if I was smart, they'd reply, 'Of course you are. You're our daughter.' Years later, when I had children of my own, I understood their logic better. Still, I remained fascinated by the idea of the truly amazing prodigy (which I never, even with parental encouragement, would have been)—an Alexander Pope, a Shirley Temple, a Mozart. Isaac Stern, the famous violinist who was *not* a prodigy, held the notion that musical prodigies had to retrain in their twenties, ridding themselves of their childish behavioral tics to be a success in the adult world. That notion has become mine, too—only I extend it to all prodigies, not just musical ones. Running through this poem are a few snatches of the lyrics from *The Mikado* of 'The Flowers That Bloom in the Spring'—a kind of paean to innocence and joy. My notion of retraining for any prodigy is to stop focusing on past triumphs and start over at 'one'—at innocence and joy, to learn to be a whole person, a non-solipsistic adult."

MICHAEL TYRELL was born in Brooklyn, New York, in 1974. He is the author of the poetry collection *The Wanted* (The National Poetry Review Press, 2012). With Julia Spicher Kasdorf, he edited *Broken Land: Poems of Brooklyn* (NYU Press, 2007). A graduate of the Iowa Writers' Workshop, he teaches at New York University.

Of "Delicatessen," Tyrell writes: "I've always been fascinated by how documentaries can make the quotidian seem mythic, and after taking in so many stories on social and other media about the aftermath of Hurricane Sandy in 2012, I found myself writing in a quasi-documentary style, taking stock of my own minor daily routines and the imagined lives of people I saw or encountered in my Brooklyn neighborhood. As the poem took shape, other figures emerged, one being Hyacinth Thrash—a survivor of the tragedy in Jonestown in 1978. Her story, which I heard recounted in a documentary, has haunted me for years. I hope I've done her justice."

WENDY VIDELOCK was born in Ohio and raised in Tucson, Arizona, where she graduated from the University of Arizona. She now lives in western Colorado, where she writes, paints, and teaches. Her books, *Nevertheless* (2011), *The Dark Gnu* (2013), and *Slingshots and Love Plums* (2015), have been published by Able Muse Press.

SIDNEY WADE's sixth collection of poems, *Straits & Narrows*, was published by Persea Books in 2013. Her translations from the Turkish, *Selected Poems of Melih Cevdet Anday*, won the Meral Divitci Prize and will be published in October 2015. She has served as president of Associated Writing Programs (AWP) and secretary/treasurer of the American Literary Translators' Association. She teaches workshops in poetry and translation at the University of Florida's MFA@FLA program. She is the poetry editor of *Subtropics*.

CODY WALKER was born in Baltimore, Maryland, in 1967. He is the author of *Shuffle and Breakdown* (Waywiser Press, 2008) and coeditor of *Alive at the Center: An Anthology of Poems from the Pacific Northwest* (Ooligan Press, 2013). He lives in Ann Arbor and teaches English at the University of Michigan. His second poetry collection, *The Self-Styled No-Child*, will be published by Waywiser in 2016.

Of "Trades I Would Make," Walker writes: "Several summers ago, I started going to an Ann Arbor café called Mighty Good. My first daughter had been born the previous fall; I'd written almost nothing in the intervening months. So my partner and I hired a babysitter, which allowed us to escape to Mighty Good on Sunday afternoons and feel like writers again. I joked that the title for my next book would be *These Poems Are Costing Me Ten Dollars an Hour*. (These days, with two kids, the poems cost thirteen dollars an hour.) 'Trades I Would Make' emerged from those carefree afternoons."

LaWanda Walters was born in Fort Worth, Texas, in 1949. Her poems have appeared in *The Antioch Review*, *The Cincinnati Review*, *The Georgia Review*, *The Laurel Review*, *North American Review*, *Ploughshares*, *Shenandoah*, and *Southern Poetry Review*. She received an MA in literature from California State University at Humboldt and an MFA in poetry from Indiana University, where she won an Academy of American Poets Prize. She lives in Cincinnati.

Of "Goodness in Mississippi," Walters writes: "My poem is a double elegy, in which I mourn and try to reconcile the early deaths of two people in very different circumstances. On the surface the poem speaks mostly about my first best friend, who amazed me with her early maturity and natural kindness and was my first role model. But the poem is also—and primarily—my acknowledgment of the near-miraculous mystery when someone chooses to be good in a place and time that makes that choice impossible. In a state that was proudest of its two Miss Mississippis, only the beautiful and the white were acknowledged. It was a hollow, superficial existence, and the spectrum of its cruelty extended from a lonely white kid with pimples and a long nose to someone who identified himself as black, like Vernon Dahmer, who lived in Hattiesburg, just as we did, and was a successful businessman, the owner of acres of farmland and a logging business. I believe that both my friend and Mr. Dahmer died because they were the 'good' in Mississippi, a place that did not hand out awards for substance, just appearance. Let me be clear that my friend did not die out of her own vanity. She genuinely cared about other people but was secretly mean to herself. So I make the leap from my friend, who was too kind, to someone neither of us knew, a man who owned a store in a separate part of town and was concerned enough about his friends, who had not managed to get past the racist registrar at the Hattiesburg Courthouse, to keep a ledger in his store for people to sign up to vote, to pay the poll taxes for those who could not afford that travesty, and to speak on a radio show (the morning before his murder) announcing the venue of his store as a safe place for people to come and sign up to vote.

"I was able to write this poem—in which I try to speak of Dahmer's sacrifice for the good of others—when I tried Terrance Hayes's 'golden shovel' form, which he invented in homage to Gwendolyn Brooks's 'We Real Cool.' I feel so grateful for that form and for the opportunity to express my white girl's humility and awe toward a heroism for which all of us can never be grateful enough.

"A longer backstory about the poem's genesis, 'Mississippi Daze,' appears on the *Georgia Review* website: garev.uga.edu/wordpress/index. php/2014/04/mississip pi-daze/."

Born in 1951, AFAA MICHAEL WEAVER was the firstborn of five children of black working-class parents who came north to Baltimore, Maryland, from the family homeland in Brunswick County, Virginia, and Northampton County, North Carolina. Encouraged by his parents, he skipped the eighth grade and entered the University of Maryland's main campus at College Park in 1968 when he was sixteen years old. After completing two years in good standing there, he returned to Baltimore and worked in factories from 1970 to 1985, during which time he wrote poetry, short fiction, and newspaper articles. During those years he also founded 7th Son Press and published the journal *Blind Alleys*. He left factory life in 1985 with an NEA fellowship in poetry and a contract for his first book, *Water Song* (Callaloo). He completed his BA (1986) at the State University of New York and did his graduate work (1985–1987) at Brown. He has published thirteen more collections of poetry, most recently *A Hard Summation* (Central Square Press, 2014) and *City of Eternal Spring* (University of Pittsburgh Press, 2014). His twelfth collection, *The Government of Nature*, received the 2014 Kingsley Tufts Award. He has a first-degree black sash in Taijiquan and is a Dao disciple in the Tien Shan Pai Association. He lives in Somerville, Massachusetts. He adapted his birth name, Michael Schan Weaver, in 1998 when he used "Afaa" for his sixth poetry collection, *Talisman* (Tia Chucha). His websites are afaaweaver.net and plumflowertrilogy.org.

Weaver writes: " 'City of Eternal Spring' is the title poem from my most recent collection of poetry, the book that completes my Plum Flower Trilogy that began with *The Plum Flower Dance* and includes *The Government of Nature*. This title poem from *City of Eternal Spring* takes as its subject the Daoist strategy of working toward emptiness in sitting meditation and in the application of new consciousness acquired in meditation toward the business of daily living and the exploration of self and experience.

" 'City of Eternal Spring' also refers to the heart, which in Chinese is represented by the character xin 心 and also means 'mind.' In Daoist contemplative life, the realization of the heart and mind as one is preliminary to working toward emptiness. In that way the poem celebrates release from the entanglement of trauma and trauma repetition, a victory in that my life is no longer so deeply circumscribed by the trauma and by its effects.

"The poem establishes imagery of the mind as architectural structure, one that is both filled and transformed by the process of healing from childhood sexual abuse through healing contexts established in intersections with Chinese culture. The mind as architectural structure with consciousness formed in light and the tiniest specks of electromagnetic energy driven by the body's considerable electricity have formed a central metaphor for my work over the last ten years. It emerges from my Daoist studies and a foundation in math, science, architecture, and engineering I received early in life."

CANDACE G. WILEY is cofounder and codirector of The Watering Hole, an online community dedicated to poets of color. She was born in 1985 and raised between small towns in rural South Carolina, where there were more cattle than people and no need for stoplights. She received her BA from Bowie State University (the first Maryland HBCU), her MA from Clemson University, and her MFA at the University of South Carolina. She has served as the creative writing director for a production of the musical revue *Jacques Brel: Alive and Well and Living in Paris*, which was a benefit performance for Haiti, and she has written dialogues and poetry for the prototype of Ghosts of South Carolina College, an iPhone app that shows the enslaved people who built and maintained antebellum USC. She has recently returned to the United States after conducting research in San Basilio de Palenque, Colombia, as a Fulbright Fellow. Palenque is one of the many towns founded by escaped slaves in the 1600s—and the only one that still exists in Colombia. The people have their own language as well as customs that trace back to the Bantu and Kikongo in West Africa. She teaches in South Carolina.

On "Dear Black Barbie," Wiley writes: "While in the process of going through Denise Duhamel's *Kinky*, I needed to add bits of my own childhood perception of Barbie to the conversation. Although I grew up well loved by my African American community, saw many of its members as beautiful and handsome, and had a healthy sense of self, I still had a very complex relationship to skin. Later, as an undergraduate student at Bowie State University, a Historically Black University, I met many other young women who were willing to admit shameful childhood propensities toward whiteness as the standard of beauty—shameful because we were young, revolutionary, decidedly black, and millennial—although we still had to reassert and re-remind ourselves, and each other, of our own inherent beauty. This state of unrecognized beauty worked with the hypersexualization of Barbie to the extent that it opened a young girl, who did not fully know that sex existed, to create her own childhood lesbian erotica following the idea that if Ken couldn't love Barbie, someone had to.

"With this poem, I was able to take a real childhood memory and pair it with my own adult commentary about the very historical lightening and blond-ing of African American women whose beauty is to be admired as it is and the masculinization of those who do not fit the aforementioned categories of the 'beautiful.' Each is a ticket that costs something. This poem asks: Have African American women earned the right to 'womanhood' and have we really progressed?"

TERENCE WINCH's most recent books are *This Way Out* (Hanging Loose Press, 2014), *Lit from Below* (Salmon Poetry [Ireland], 2013), and *Falling Out of Bed in a Room with No Floor* (Hanging Loose, 2011). He has received an American Book Award, a grant from the National Endowment for the Arts, and a Gertrude Stein Award for innovative writing. Born in the Bronx, New York, he has lived in the Washington, DC, area for many years. He has played traditional Irish music all his life.

Of "Subject to Change," Winch writes: "I have been writing a lot of sonnets in the past year or two, so much so that even when I don't set out to write a sonnet, I somehow wind up with a fourteen-line poem. I think that's what happened with this poem. Change—what the Romantics called 'mutability'—is one of the great subjects of poetry, right up there with sex and death. We are always trying to elude what Wordsworth called 'the unimaginable touch of Time,' and I think this poem is a protest against the ways in which we are ruthlessly measured by the passage of time."

JANE WONG was born in New Jersey in 1984. The recipient of fellowships from the U.S. Fulbright Program, the Bread Loaf Writers' Conference, Kundiman, Squaw Valley, and the Fine Arts Work Center, she holds an MFA from the Iowa Writers' Workshop. She teaches at the University of Washington and the Richard Hugo House in Seattle.

Wong writes: "'Thaw' is a poem for the New Year—a proclamation of warmth and messiness. H.D.'s early work feels tied to this poem; she writes in 'Oread': 'hurl your green over us, / cover us with your pools of fir.' I wanted that feeling of impossible warmth and potential, hurling us into each new day."

MONICA YOUN is the author of *Blackacre* (Graywolf Press, 2016), *Ignatz* (Four Way Books, 2010), which was a finalist for the National Book Award, and *Barter* (Graywolf Press, 2003). She received her AB from Princeton University, her MPhil in English literature from Oxford University, where she was a Rhodes Scholar, and her JD from Yale Law School. She practiced law for more than a decade, testifying before Congress on multiple occasions, appearing as an expert commentator on PBS and MSNBC, and publishing political commentary in *Slate* and *The New York Times*. Her poems have appeared in *The New York Times Magazine*, *The New Yorker*, and *The Paris Review*. She has been awarded the Wallace Stegner Fellowship at Stanford University and the Witter Bynner Fellowship of the Library of Congress. She currently teaches poetry at Princeton University's Lewis Center for the Arts and in the MFA program for writers at Warren Wilson College.

Of "March of the Hanged Men," Youn writes: "This poem is part of a series loosely based on François Villon's fifteenth-century poem 'Ballade des pendus' ('Ballad of the Hanged Men'). Villon's poem is in the voice of a group of corpses hanging from a gibbet in the town square, describing their processes of bodily decomposition and praying for human forgiveness and divine absolution. The figure of the hanged man also features in multiple religious and cultural traditions, often signifying a moment of transformation into a predestined role. This particular poem draws from my residency at the Civitella Ranieri Foundation in Umbertide, Italy, where, on successive days, I saw the ants described in the poem as well as Piero della Francesca's great painting *The Resurrection* in the nearby town of San Sepolcro."

MAGAZINES WHERE THE POEMS
WERE FIRST PUBLISHED

Able Muse, poetry ed. Alexander Pepple. www.ablemuse.com

The Academy of American Poets, Poem-a-Day series, ed. Alex Dimitrov. www.poets.org

Alaska Quarterly Review, editor-in-chief Ronald Spatz. University of Alaska Anchorage, 3211 Providence Drive, Anchorage, AK 99508. www.uaa.alaska.edu/aqr/

The American Poetry Review, eds. David Bonanno and Elizabeth Scanlon. 320 S. Broad St., Hamilton #313, Philadelphia, PA 19102. www.aprweb.org

The Atlantic Monthly, poetry ed. David Barber. The Watergate, 600 New Hampshire Ave., NW, Washington, DC 20037.

The Awl, poetry ed. Mark Bibbins. www.theawl.com

Beltway Poetry Quarterly, ed. Kim Roberts. www.beltwaypoetry.com

Birdfeast, editor-in-chief Jessica Poli. www.birdfeastmagazine.com

Blackbird, an online journal of literature and the arts, senior eds. Gregory Donovan and Mary Flinn. www.blackbird.vcu.edu

Burrow Press Review, ed. Ryan Rivas and guest poetry ed. Erica Dawson. www.burrowpressreview.com

The Carolina Quarterly, poetry ed. Lee Norton. 510 Greenlaw Hall CB# 3520, The University of North Carolina at Chapel Hill, Chapel Hill, NC 27599-3520. www.thecarolinaquarterly.com/

The Cincinnati Review, poetry ed. Don Bogen. PO Box 210069, Cincinnati, OH 45221-0069. www.cincinnatireview.com

Colorado Review, poetry eds. Donald Revell, Sasha Steensen, and Matthew Cooperman. Department of English, Colorado State University, Fort Collins, CO 80523-9105. www.coloradoreview.colostate.edu/colorado-review

Columbia Poetry Review, eds. John Bishop, Abigail Zimmer, James Eidson, Tyler Cain Lacy, David A. Moran, Christopher Neely, Daniel Scott Parker, Victoria A. Sanz, Matthew Sharos, Amy Jo Trier-Walker, and Gabrielle Faith Williams. www.colum.edu/columbiapoetryreview

Conduit, ed. William Waltz. 788 Osceola Avenue, Saint Paul, MN 55105. www.conduit.org

Court Green, eds. CM Burroughs, Tony Trigilio, and David Trinidad. Department of Creative Writing, Columbia College Chicago, 600 South Michigan Ave., Chicago, IL 60605. www.colum.edu/court green

Denver Quarterly, poetry ed. Bin Ramke. University of Denver, Department of English, 2000 E. Asbury, Denver, CO 80208. www.du.edu/denverquarterly/

Fence, poetry eds. Brian Blanchfield, Max Winter, Farid Matuk, Charles Valle, Mendi Lewis Obadike, and Rebecca Wolff. www.fenceportal .org

Fruita Pulp, ed. Kyle Harvey. www.fruitapulp.com

The Georgia Review, ed. Stephen Corey. Main Library, Room 706A, 320 S. Jackson St., The University of Georgia, Athens, GA 30602-9009. garev.uga.edu

Granta, poetry ed. Rachael Allen. www.granta.com

Harper's, "Readings" ed. Giles Harvey. www.harpers.org

The Hopkins Review, eds. John T. Irwin, Brad Leithauser, Alice McDermott, Jean McGarry, Mary Jo Salter, Dave Smith, and David Yezzi. The Writing Seminars, Johns Hopkins University, 3400 North Charles St., Baltimore, MD 21218. www.thehopkinsreview.com

The Iowa Review, poetry eds. Nikki-Lee Birdsey and Anthony Cinquepalmi. 308 EPB, University of Iowa, Iowa City, IA 52242. www .iowareview.org

The Journal, poetry eds. Megan Peak and David Winter. www.thejournal mag.org

The Kenyon Review, poetry ed. David Baker. www.kenyonreview.org

Kinfolks Quarterly, poetry eds. Jerriod Avant, Aziza Barnes, Joshua Bennett, Sean DesVignes, Safia Elhillo, Eve Ewing, Nate Marshall, and Lauren Yates. www.kinfolksquarterly.com

Lemon Hound, ed. Sina Queyras. www.lemonhound.com

The Literary Review, poetry ed. Craig Morgan Teicher. www.theliterary review.org

The Manhattan Review, ed. Philip Fried. 440 Riverside Drive #38, New York, NY 10027. www.themanhattanreview.com

Muzzle, editor-in-chief Stevie Edwards; poetry eds. Benjamin Clark and Laura Swearingen-Steadwell. www.muzzlemagazine.com

The New Criterion, poetry ed. David Yezzi. 900 Broadway, Suite 602, New York, NY 10003. www.newcriterion.com

New Ohio Review, ed. Jill Allyn Rosser. English Dept., 360 Ellis Hall, Ohio University, Athens, OH 45701. www.ohio.edu/nor/

The New Yorker, poetry ed. Paul Muldoon. 1 World Trade Center, New York, NY 10007. www.newyorker.com

Ninth Letter, poetry ed. Michael Madonick. University of Illinois, Dept. of English, 608 South Wright St., Urbana, IL 61801. www.ninth letter.com

PANK, eds. Colin Winnette, Roxane Gay, and M. Bartley Seigel. www .pankmagazine.com

The Paris Review, poetry ed. Robyn Creswell. 544 W. 27th St., New York, NY 10001. www.theparisreview.org

Pleiades, poetry eds. Wayne Miller and Kathryn Nuernberger. www .ucmo.edu/pleiades/

PMS poemmemoirstory, poetry ed. Halley Cotton. www.uab.edu/cas/ englishpublications/pms-poemmemoirstory

Poetry, ed. Don Share. www.poetryfoundation.org

Poetry Daily, eds. Don Selby and Diane Boller. www.poems.com

Poetry Northwest, ed. Kevin Craft. www.poetrynw.org

Post Road, guest ed. Suzanne Matson. www.postroadmag.com

Powder Keg, eds. Zoe Dzunko and Sarah Jean Grimm. www.powder kegmagazine.com

Prairie Schooner, assistant editors: poetry, Arden Eli Hill and Rebecca Macijeski. 123 Andrews Hall, University of Nebraska, Lincoln, NE 68588-0334. www.prairieschooner.unl.edu

A Public Space, poetry ed. Brett Fletcher Lauer. www.apublicspace.org

Rattle, eds. Alan Fox and Timothy Green. 12411 Ventura Blvd., Studio City, CA 91604. www.rattle.com

The Rumpus, poetry ed. Brian Spears. www.therumpus.net

The Southampton Review, poetry ed. Julie Sheehan. www.stonybrook .edu/southampton/mfa/publishing/tsr.html

The Southern Review, poetry ed. Jessica Faust. Louisiana State University, 338 Johnston Hall, Baton Rouge, LA 70803. www.thesouthern review.org

Southwest Review, editor-in-chief Willard Spiegelman. PO Box 750374, Dallas, TX 75275-0374. www.smu.edu/SouthwestReview

Subtropics, poetry ed. Sidney Wade. www.subtropics.english.ufl.edu

32 Poems, ed. George David Clark; associate eds. Susanna Childress, Nick McRae, Matt Morton, and Michael Shewmaker. Valparaiso University, 1320 Chapel Drive South, Valparaiso, IN 46383. www .32poems.com

The Threepenny Review, ed. Wendy Lesser. PO Box 9131, Berkeley, CA 94709. www.threepennyreview.com

Tupelo Quarterly, senior poetry eds. T. J. Jarrett, Katherine Durham Oldmixon, and Stacey Waite. www.tupeloquarterly.com

Unsplendid, eds. Douglas Basford, Jason Gray, and Ida Stewart. www .unsplendid.com

upstreet, poetry ed. Jessica Greenbaum. upstreet-mag.org/

Verse Daily, eds. Hunter Hamilton and Campbell Russo. www.versedaily .org

The Volta, eds. Afton Wilky and Joshua Marie Wilkinson. www.thevolta .org

West Branch, ed. G. C. Waldrep. www.bucknell.edu/westbranch

ACKNOWLEDGMENTS

The series editor thanks Mark Bibbins for his invaluable assistance. Warm thanks go also to Nora Brooks, Danielle Chin, and Stacey Harwood; to Glen Hartley and Lynn Chu of Writers' Representatives; and to Ashley Gilliam, David Stanford Burr, Daniel Cuddy, Erich Hobbing, and Gwyneth Stansfield at Scribner.

Grateful acknowledgment is made of the magazines in which these poems first appeared and the magazine editors who selected them. A sincere attempt has been made to locate all copyright holders. Unless otherwise noted, copyright to the poems is held by the individual poets.

Sarah Arvio, "Bodhisattva" from the Academy of American Poets' Poem-a-Day series. Reprinted by permission of the poet.

Derrick Austin, "Cedars of Lebanon" from *Burrow Press Review*. Reprinted by permission of the poet.

Desiree Bailey, "A Retrograde" from *Muzzle*. Reprinted by permission of the poet.

Melissa Barrett, "WFM: Allergic to Pine-Sol, Am I the Only One" from *The Journal*. Reprinted by permission of the poet.

Mark Bibbins, "Swallowed" from *Lemon Hound*. Reprinted by permission of the poet.

Jessamyn Birrer, "A Scatology" from *Ninth Letter*. Reprinted by permission of the poet.

Chana Bloch, "The Joins" from *The Southern Review* and *Poetry Daily*. Reprinted by permission of the poet.

Emma Bolden, "House Is an Enigma" from *Conduit*. Reprinted by permission of the poet.

Dexter L. Booth, "Prayer at 3 a.m." from *The Volta*. Reprinted by permission of the poet.

Catherine Bowman, "Makeshift" from *The New Yorker*. Reprinted by permission of the poet.

Rachael Briggs, "in the hall of the ruby-throated warbler" from *Able Muse*. Reprinted by permission of the poet.

Jericho Brown, "Homeland" from *Fence*. Reprinted by permission of the poet.

Rafael Campo, "DOCTORS LIE, MAY HIDE MISTAKES" from *upstreet*. Reprinted by permission of the poet.

Julie Carr, "A fourteen-line poem on sex" from *The Kenyon Review*. Reprinted by permission of the poet.

Chen Chen, "for i will do/undo what was done/undone to me" from *PANK*. Reprinted by permission of the poet.

Susanna Childress, "Careful, I Just Won a Prize at the Fair" from *Columbia Poetry Review*. Reprinted by permission of the poet.

Yi-Fen Chou, "The Bees, the Flowers, Jesus, Ancient Tigers, Poseidon, Adam and Eve" from *Prairie Schooner*. Reprinted by permission of Michael Derrick Hudson.

Erica Dawson, "Slow-Wave Sleep with a Fairy Tale" from *Tupelo Quarterly*. Reprinted by permission of the poet.

Danielle DeTiberus, "In a Black Tank Top" from *Rattle*. Reprinted by permission of the poet.

Natalie Diaz, "It Was the Animals" from *Poetry*. Reprinted by permission of the poet.

Denise Duhamel, "Fornicating" from *The Literary Review*. Reprinted by permission of the poet.

Thomas Sayers Ellis, "Vernacular Owl" from *Poetry*. Reprinted by permission of the poet.

Emily Kendal Frey, "In Memory of My Parents Who Are Not Dead Yet" from *Powder Keg*. Reprinted by permission of the poet.

James Galvin, "On the Sadness of Wedding Dresses" from *The Iowa Review*. Reprinted by permission of the poet.

Madelyn Garner, "The Garden in August" from *PMS: poemmemoirstory*. Reprinted by permission of the poet.

Amy Gerstler, "Rhinencephalon" from *The American Poetry Review*. Reprinted by permission of the poet.

Louise Glück, "A Sharply Worded Silence" from *Faithful and Virtuous Night*. © 2014 by Louise Glück. Reprinted by permission of Farrar, Straus and Giroux. Also appeared in *The Threepenny Review*.

R. S. Gwynn, "Looney Tunes" from *Dogwatch*. © 2014 by R. S. Gwynn. Reprinted by permission of Measure Press. Also appeared in *Able Muse*.

Meredith Hasemann, "Thumbs" from *The Southampton Review*. Reprinted by permission of the poet.

Jamaal May, "There Are Birds Here" from *Poetry*. Reprinted by permission of the poet.

Laura McCullough, "There Were Only Dandelions" from *Rigger Death & Hoist Another*. © 2013 by Laura McCullough. Reprinted by permission of Black Lawrence Press. Also appeared on *Verse Daily*.

Rajiv Mohabir, "Dove" from *Prairie Schooner*. Reprinted by permission of the poet.

Aimee Nezhukumatathil, "Upon Hearing the News You Buried Our Dog" from the Academy of American Poets' Poem-a-Day series.

D. Nurkse, "Plutonium" from *The Manhattan Review*. Reprinted by permission of the poet.

Tanya Olson, "54 Prince" from *The Awl*. Reprinted by permission of the poet.

Ron Padgett, "Survivor Guilt" from *Alone and Not Alone*. © 2015 by Ron Padgett. Reprinted with the permission of The Permissions Company, Inc., on behalf of Coffee House Press. Also appeared in the Academy of American Poets' Poem-a-Day series.

Alan Michael Parker, "Candying Mint" from *The Carolina Quarterly*. Reprinted by permission of the poet.

Catherine Pierce, "Relevant Details" from *Pleiades*. Reprinted by permission of the poet.

Donald Platt, "The Main Event" from *Southwest Review*. Reprinted by permission of the poet.

Claudia Rankine, from *Citizen*. © 2014 by Claudia Rankine. Reprinted with the permission of The Permissions Company, Inc., on behalf of Graywolf Press. Also appeared in *Granta*.

Raphael Rubinstein, "Poem Begun on a Train" from *Harper's*. Reprinted by permission of the poet.

Natalie Scenters-Zapico, "Endnotes on Ciudad Juárez" from *West Branch*. Reprinted by permission of the poet.

Evie Shockley, "legend" from *Fence*. Reprinted by permission of the poet.

Charles Simic, "So Early in the Morning" from *The Paris Review*. Reprinted by permission of the poet.

Sandra Simonds, "Similitude at Versailles" from *Colorado Review*. Reprinted by permission of the poet.

Ed Skoog, "The Macarena" from *Fruita Pulp*. Reprinted by permission of the poet.

A. E. Stallings, "Ajar" from *The Atlantic Monthly*. Reprinted by permission of the poet.

Susan Terris, "Memo to the Former Child Prodigy" from *Denver Quarterly*. Reprinted by permission of the poet.

Michael Tyrell, "Delicatessen" from *The Iowa Review*. Reprinted by permission of the poet.

Wendy Videlock, "How You Might Approach a Foal:" from *The New Criterion*. Reprinted by permission of the poet.

Sidney Wade, "The Chickasaw Trees" from *Blackbird: an online journal of literature and the arts*. Reprinted by permission of the poet.

Cody Walker, "Trades I Would Make" from *Poetry Northwest*. Reprinted by permission of the poet.

LaWanda Walters, "Goodness in Mississippi" from *The Georgia Review*. Reprinted by permission of the poet.

Afaa Michael Weaver, "City of Eternal Spring" from *City of Eternal Spring*. © 2014 by Afaa Michael Weaver. Reprinted by permission of the University of Pittsburgh Press. Also appeared in *The Rumpus*.

Candace G. Wiley, "Dear Black Barbie" from *Prairie Schooner*. Reprinted by permission of the poet.

Terence Winch, "Subject to Change" from *Beltway Poetry Quarterly*. Reprinted by permission of the poet.

Jane Wong, "Thaw" from *Birdfeast*. Reprinted by permission of the poet.

Monica Youn, "March of the Hanged Men" from *The Paris Review*. Reprinted by permission of the poet.